THE GODDESS REMEDY

Unleash Your Power,
Embody Your Truth, and
Love Without Limits

THE GODDESS REMEDY

SUZIN GREEN

SHE WRITES PRESS

Published in 2026 by
She Writes Press, an imprint of The Stable Book Group

32 Court Street, Suite 2109
Brooklyn, NY 11201
https://shewritespress.com

Library of Congress Control Number: 2025917169
ISBN: 979-8-89636-046-9
eISBN: 979-8-89636-047-6

Interior designer: Katherine Lloyd, The DESK

Printed in the United States

Names and identifying characteristics have been changed to protect the privacy of certain individuals.

For Michael Brooks

1983–2020

Rest in love, MB, always in love . . .

With the pincers of truth I have plucked
From the dark corners of my heart
The thorn of many judgments.
I sit in my own splendor. . . .

I sit in my own radiance,
And I have no fear.

Waking,
Dreaming,
Sleeping,
What are they to me?

Or even ecstasy? . . .
I sit in my own splendor

Dissolving the mind,
Or the highest meditation,
The world and all its works . . .
What are they to me?

I sit in my own radiance.

Why talk of wisdom,
The three ends of life,
Or oneness?

Why talk of these!

Now I live in my heart.

—Ashtavakra Gita

CONTENTS

PART III: THE GODDESS RULES
SIX PRACTICES FOR BECOMING YOUR MOST AMAZING SELF

PREFACE

Gina comes in for a session. Trapped in a vortex of anxiety, she can't sleep, can't eat, can't focus. I listen for a while and then suggest we stop talking and sit quietly together. She's resistant. The anxiety has her convinced that if she lets herself be drawn out of its grip, something bad will happen. This is partially true. Something "bad" will happen. To the anxiety. It will dissolve.

We've worked together for a long time. She trusts me enough to sit back, close her eyes, and begin to feel her breath. It's that simple. I watch the tightness in her face soften. I hear her breath stretch longer. I sense her shift out of the contracted mind space she's been crammed into. Now the whole room fills with stillness and she is home.

The Great Myth of Our Time

The great myth of our time is that we're separate from one another—isolated individuals trapped in a zero-sum game based on survival of the fittest. When we step through this veil, we realize we're part of something much greater; that this whole business of individual this and individual that, of domination and accumulation as the goal of human life, is absurd.

We've been tricked into believing we have to be more, do more, strive after that elusive more, which no matter how close we get to it always eludes us. This is a lie. When we slow ourselves down, pushing back against the compulsion to do more, be more, strive more, we discover a simple truth: that even in all our wounding and muddle, we are enough. And that rather than seeking outside ourselves for the everything we think is there, what we really need to do is turn within and listen.

> Rather than seeking outside ourselves for the everything we think is there, what we really need to do is turn within and listen.

This is not to say we should withdraw from the world. On the contrary. The world very much needs us. It needs us awake. It needs us engaged. It needs us understanding that the answers to the great longings of life are not outside us, have never been outside us, will never be outside us—and anyone who says they are is wrong.

INTRODUCTION

Just sit there right now.
Don't do a thing.
Just rest . . .

For your separation from God
Is the hardest work in this world.

Let me bring you trays of food
And something
That you like to drink.

You can use my soft words

As a cushion
For your
Head.
—Hafiz/Ladinsky

Welcome.

Of all the self-help books you might have picked up to listen to or read, I'm so glad you chose this one. I can't promise it will answer every question or solve every problem. No book can do that. I do, however, believe that working with the ideas contained here will give you fresh new ways of understanding yourself and your place in the world.

A note about some of the terms you'll encounter. Words like "patriarchy" and "goddess" may ping for you. Please bear with me if they do. Language is powerful, and I use these words with intention. In the case of "patriarchy," it's a necessary evil for making necessary points. In the case of "goddess," well, I suspect you'll come around.

Part I takes a deep dive into what you might think of as the inner meaning of patriarchy. Rest assured, we'll be thinking about that trigger of a word in a whole new way. Regardless of your gender identification, I suspect you'll find the content here intriguing, and hopefully much more than that.

In Part II we go the other way, reveling in the multilateral mystery that is the Goddess. And again, regardless of your gender ID or incredulity, you may well discover a glorious gleaming goddess shining deep inside your heart.

And then we come to Part III. I know the wise ones say, "The joy is in the journey, not the destination," but truth be told, I am excited for you to reach this particular destination. I'm not suggesting you jump ahead. In fact, the best way to read this book is to take a slow, thoughtful amble through all that comes before it. But the six practices of Part III, the Goddess Rules, are solid gold. Take them into your awareness. Embody them throughout your day. This simple act can guide you toward becoming your most amazing self. And that is a promise I can make.

May you take rest here. May this book be a cushion for your head. And may the doors of limitless possibility break open inside you.

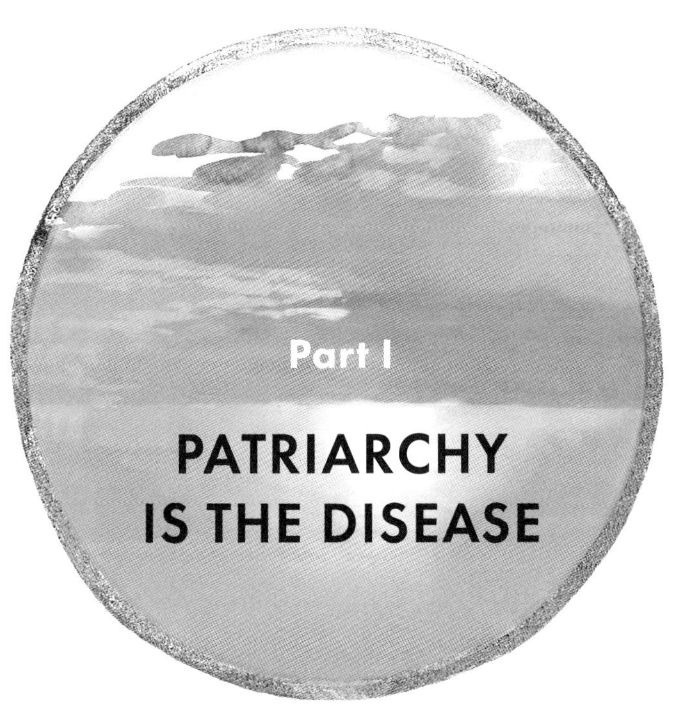

Part I

PATRIARCHY IS THE DISEASE

Jack and Jill went up the hill
to fetch a pail of water
Jack fell down and broke his crown
and Jill came tumbling after.

All of humanity's problems stem from man's inability
to sit quietly in a room alone.
—Blaise Pascal

Chapter 1

THE JOURNEY

When Francis Hardwood, an anthropologist,
asked a Sioux elder why people tell stories, he answered:
"In order to become human beings."
She asked, "Aren't we human beings already?"
He smiled. "Not everyone makes it."
—Laura Simms

I was born on April 22, 1948, at the Queen of the Angels Hospital in Los Angeles, California. The due date was June 6, but there were complications and I was delivered six weeks early. I weighed four pounds, six ounces and was missing eyelashes and fingernails, so they kept me in the incubator until I'd grown to term.

When I was a little girl, my mother would tell me stories of the neonatal nurses who cared for me, stories that made a strong impression on my young mind. I think it was something about a group of women working in a hospital called Queen of the Angels, women who nurtured me when my own mother could not, that touched me very deeply. Much later, as I came to see the feminine ground as essential medicine for our time, I wondered if my entry into the world is what opened my eyes to the deeper meaning of the goddess.

My parents were first-generation Americans. White. Jewish. New Yorkers. They met in 1944, soon after my father's release from serving over a decade in prison. Wanting to make a fresh start, they headed west to California and went to work in the national mobilization known as the war effort. A year later, the war ended. Three years after that, I came into the world. And a few years after that, in the booming postwar economy, one of my dad's brothers offered him a business opportunity, and they returned to New York in pursuit of the American dream.

My father's incarceration was a huge skeleton in the family closet. No one ever spoke of it. It was not until the end of his life—and he lived into his eighties—that I discovered his carefully guarded secret. Growing up white in the 1950s and '60s offered my sister and me a comfortable middle-class life. My parents built that business opportunity into a successful mail-order company, enabling us to live in a large home in a gracious suburban neighborhood. Our dad was one of six siblings, our mother one of three, so along with good friends and lovely neighbors, we had many aunts and uncles and plenty of cousins to play with. Our parents also had a wide social circle, so there were always fun and interesting people around. It was, in many ways, a good life. Yet I often had a sense that there was something wrong. I felt this most acutely with my dad's family. Something in my child's awareness sensed that we were outsiders, that he was the pariah of the clan.

The Secret

Years later, when I discovered the secret that had pervaded his adult life; when I learned how desperation for money during the Great Depression led him to take a job as a hit man for a group of neighborhood thugs, an adventure that sent them to the electric chair and him to Sing Sing and Dannemora prisons; when I learned how that scandalous event had shamed his entire family, it all made sense. We *were* the outsiders and he *was* the pariah.

His family never fully forgave him. Worse than that, I don't think he ever forgave himself. I think he lived with an unspeakable shame, and the consequences of that shame rippled out from him onto my mother, my sister, and me. I've long believed that what drew me to study Eastern philosophy, Western psychology, and the healing power of the arts, and to eventually earn my living as a wisdom teacher, therapist, and coach, was not just my own longing for healing and transformation but also a deep, unconscious longing to heal my father.

I still remember a summer afternoon when I was five years old. I was outside playing with my dad. He was teaching me to jump rope. The sun was shining and all was right in my young world. Then, suddenly, the weather changed, the sky turned gray, and I saw what looked like a dark cloud all around him. There was something sinister about it that scared me.

A few minutes later it started to rain and we went back inside. I waited until he'd gone into the kitchen, then slipped into the den where no one would hear me, picked up the telephone, and called God, asking "him" to help my father. My parents were atheists. The word "God" was never spoken in our home. I have no idea why I thought I could phone this "God" person and that "he" would help. I just didn't know who else to call.

Although all I actually heard was the dial tone, I sensed a comforting presence listening, and my concerns slowly eased. I was way too young in my journey to understand that the comforting presence I met that day was the me inside of me, the "me" who would grow into the artist, teacher, and healer that I became.

Planting the Seeds

I started playing the piano when I was six years old. My childhood piano, a mahogany baby grand, has been my traveling companion ever since. It has been the record keeper and solace provider of my life. It's where I learned to play the classical keyboard literature and taught myself to improvise; where I found my own musical voice, and had the mind-altering experience that plunged me onto the spiritual path. It's where I spent the better part of several decades practicing, composing, performing, and collaborating with other artists and where I've taught the arts of music and living to so many people. It's where countless seeds for the work I do today were planted.

More of those seeds took root in 1977, when, after several years of exploring Eastern and Western wisdom traditions, I attended a meditation retreat taught by senior disciples of a revered Indian guru. The retreat was held over the four days of Thanksgiving weekend, and from the moment I walked in the door, I was home. Although the guru himself was in India at the time, his larger-than-life presence was palpable. I loved everything. The stillness of the meditation. The bliss of the chanting. The genius of the teachings. The attention to beauty. The intellectual depth. The moments of hilarity. The scintillating energy field—they called it the shakti—that pervaded the place. For the next seventeen years I was wholly devoted to this guru and his path.

I devoured the Tantric and Vedic texts he taught us, fell in love with the mystical poets he quoted, adopted a rigorous schedule of meditation and mantra practice in our home, and helped grow the community of devotees in our town. Whenever I could, I took off for weekends and extended retreats at his ashrams in New York, Ann Arbor, Boston, and Oakland. I revered our guru as an omniscient master at the top of the spiritual hierarchy, a fully enlightened human being who would open the door to inner liberation.

The teachings told us that worshipping the guru was the supreme path; that surrendering our ego to him was the highest practice; that the guru was the grace-bestowing power of God, and that his presence in our lives was the greatest possible blessing.

And then, nearly two decades later, the ground of my belief system exploded, and when the dust settled, I could no longer live within the paradigm of a guru-centric tradition. It simply made no sense. I could love and honor a teacher, yes, but worshipping another human being seemed at best counterproductive, and at worst a dangerous exercise in giving my power away.

Leaving the Guru

Leaving the guru was a complex endeavor. I never doubted the beauty and wisdom inherent in the yogic tradition. I just knew that I had to examine the teachings I'd imbibed over nearly two decades, separating fact from fiction. This required cutting through layers of projection and magical thinking that had grown around me like a second skin. Stripping away these veils was strangely akin to discovering my father's big secret. That had been initially shocking, but was mostly confirming of a long-held intuitive sense. It hadn't rocked my world. This, though, was a free fall. Taking back my power required me to stand alone in the ground of my own experience. There was no more organizational safety net to fall back on, no more community to be part of, no more belief system to believe in, no more great being who had my back—there was only me.

That belief system was a lovely structure. It gave me many deep, rich years. It was only after the lock was sprung that I realized there'd even been a lock. Any belief system, no matter how sublime, keeps us wrapped inside the structures of that system.

Waking up, it seems, often begins with a great shattering.

I look around me today and see shattering everywhere—starting with our broken planet and moving out through every system, animal, vegetable, mineral, human and not-human, village, town, city, state, country, and beyond. And the thing that strikes me over and over again is that we cannot heal this broken world without also healing the broken places inside ourselves. Like it or not, inner and outer are intimately connected, bound together in the evolutionary project we think of as our lives.

> We cannot heal this broken world without also healing the broken places inside ourselves.

Until we reach a tipping point of people working on inner and outer, not one or other but both together—even though the messes of this world may sometimes appear to be mending—I fear that things will stay pretty much the same. We really must shatter the tired old paradigm that has brought us here.

Chapter 2

HUMAN BEINGS AND HUMAN DOINGS

There is
A madman inside of you
Who is always running for office—
Why vote him in,
For he never keeps the accounts straight.
He gets all kinds of crooked deals
Happening all over town
That will just give you a big headache
And . . . a gigantic confused frown.
—Hafiz/Ladinsky

The 1970s ushered in a cultural zeitgeist. Sociopolitical, cultural, and spiritual mores we'd accepted seemingly forever were being challenged across the board. The deadening consequences of five thousand years of a patriarchal world order—an order defined by conquest, war, domination, hierarchy, greed, and (mostly) white male supremacy—were in the crosshairs of change. We wanted new models for living in harmony with each other and the earth.

One of the important voices of that time was Marija Gimbutas, an anthropologist studying the Neolithic and Bronze Age cultures of "Old Europe." Her research showed that once upon a time in what is now Southern Europe, there were complex societies organized around worship of the Great Goddess. Writing about it today, it seems like a big "whatever." Back in the '70s, however, it was revelatory. Gimbutas's books helped fuel the paradigm shift that was already under way, affirming the radical claim that the notion of masculine supremacy was simply not true; that the "Father God" had a partner and her name was "Mother of the Universe"; and most important, that if the planet would survive, hierarchical rankings like man over woman, mind over matter, doing over being, had to be replaced by a partnership model based on linking, not ranking; on power together, not power over; on integration, not separation; and on the undeniable fact of our planetary interdependence.

This paradigm shift was the force behind the dramatic social changes that characterized those final decades of the twentieth century. For those of us privileged enough to live this dream, these were hopeful times. It seemed that five thousand years of patriarchal evolution had come to an end. The paradigm shift, what some called the Great Turning, was here and the problems of the world would finally be solved.

Alas, not so fast . . .

The Inner Patriarch

Although women entering the workplace and men changing diapers made it look like patriarchy was crumbling—and writing now fifty years later, the patriarchal structures stand strong and backlash is horrifying—the fight was never woman against man. What a lot of us didn't understand back then (and still don't today) is that man, woman, trans, or nonbinary, we also have to fight the patriarchy inside of ourselves.

No matter the depth of your awareness or gender identification, the odds are there's a crusty old patriarch running around inside you, driving more of your thinking and behavior than you realize. A gross distortion of the true masculine, the inner patriarch is the voice we hear in our mind that passes judgment, casts doubt, dismisses, stymies, perseverates, obliterates, and seduces us into making really bad choices. The epitome of toxic masculinity, the inner patriarch separates us from ourselves, from other people, from all forms of life. It is genius at stressing us out, belittling our best ideas, and tricking us into staying when we should go and going when we should stay.

> No matter the depth of your awareness or gender identification, the odds are there's a crusty old patriarch running around inside you, driving more of your thinking and behavior than you realize.

When I was young in my journey, I had a reading with a spiritual adviser who came highly recommended. From the get-go, something about him—I think it was the look in his eyes and the way he sat just a bit too close—made me feel really uncomfortable. But I was so conditioned to deny my own feelings, so trained to give my power away, that rather than bolting, I sat there politely listening. He predicted a life of doom and gloom, saying he saw me trapped in a long tunnel with a dark man blocking my way.

I left feeling awful, and his image of the dark man in the tunnel haunted me for years. As time passed and none of his predictions came true, I began to understand that his psychic assault had been driven by his own wounding/wounded masculine. To put it bluntly, the dude was a predator on a power trip. I do give him credit for one thing. He saw the inner patriarch lurking in my unconscious. Disturbing as the image was, it gave me something concrete to work with when I began my own dismantling project.

Masculine = Doing / Feminine = Being

We're going into the weeds here, so please bear with me. We need to spend some time with the concepts of doing and being as we unpack the thinking that assigns doing to the masculine and being to the feminine. This is a tricky conversation because gender-based language is offensive to many people. It's also loaded, simplistic, and on its way to becoming obsolete.

Unfortunately, until patriarchy is replaced by solidarity, I'm afraid this outdated way of defining ourselves still has credence. If you find my use of gender terms annoying, my apologies. I'm not a fan of them either. The problem is, like it or not, agree with me or not, patriarchy is planted in the connective tissue of our bodies, hearts, and minds. If we want to root it out, we have to see it very clearly, right down to its toxic historical root.

Before we go any further, let me underline that while I'm presenting doing and being as distinct from one another, this is only to lay a groundwork for understanding how the inner patriarch forms. In a healthy system, masculine and feminine, circle and line, doing and being, are seamlessly connected within the mind/body whole. It's only the patriarchal disruption's valuing of masculine over feminine that throws off their natural (and essential) balance.

So, here goes . . .

The categories assigned to masculine and feminine have their genesis in what I'll call conventional male and female (or cisgender) bodies, specifically in the orientation of the sexual organs. Think of the male apparatus. It's visible, attached to the body exterior, and when called to action, moves in a linear way, growing rigid, pointing forward, and shooting sperm. Its focus is outward. Now think of the female apparatus. It's just the opposite. Nesting within the body interior, it is circle rather than line, forming eggs, receiving sperm, and gestating new life. Its placement and focus are inward.

These basics of anatomy are what link the externalizing *doing* function with the masculine and interior *being* realm with the feminine. Needless to say, in the big picture, it's way more nuanced than this. We're looking at how patriarchy forms inside us, however, and that begins with this dualistic and facile frame.

Let's start with doing. Doing is, quite simply, what we do. We think, we speak, we act, we perceive, we experience, we create, and in all these ways, move through our time on planet Earth.

Being is more mysterious. Being is the energy of insight, intelligence, and imagination, of feeling, emotion, archetype, and dream, and of that most mysterious of all inner phenomena, the inner light. While being may pulsate within us as waves or vibration, it doesn't "do" anything in the ways we think of doing. Being simply is.

The masculine is the doer, the thinker, speaker, and actor that carries (or restrains) all the stuff of being into thought, action, and form. Small example: Let's say you want to go for a run, but are also feeling some resistance to getting off the couch. Both your desire and resistance are arising from being. If your masculine doing function is a healthy one, your inner voice will get you into running clothes and out the door, and then will cheer you on until that moment when everything shifts, resistance morphs into elation, and you're in the zone. If, on the other hand, your doing function leans toward wounding, your inner voice will collude with your resistance, sending you down a couch-potato rabbit hole that generally ends in regret.

A wounding/wounded masculine function is what drives actions like putting everyone else's needs ahead of our own; avoiding paying bills or doing taxes; resisting deadlines of any kind; buying things like exercise bikes and never using them; accumulating piles of laundry, dishes, and unopened cartons from online retailers; or spending way too much time glued to our electronic devices. It's also what drives way more dangerous forms of cruelty and self-harm.

If you resist doing what you need (and actually want) to be doing, understand your resistance is not because you're lazy, unmotivated, disorganized, ADHD, or whatever litany of criticisms you've been led to believe is wrong with you. There is nothing wrong with you. The problem is your inner patriarch aka your wounding/wounded or broken masculine function. Its voice may seem to be you. You may believe it is you. It may be driving much of your thinking and action. It is not, however, you. It is an aberration.

The Wounding/Wounded Masculine Is *Not Your Friend*

Take this in. The compulsions that move us into destructive behaviors are driven by a broken "doing" function working overtime to trick us into causing harm to ourselves, to others, and to our planet. Instead of doing its job of holding us strong and wise, and of pushing us away from causing harm, it channels our despair, loneliness, hurt, or fear and uses these emotions, literally weaponizing them against us, to seduce us into acting against ourselves and other people. And since we're formed and deformed in patriarchy, we all have a wounding/wounded masculine sitting somewhere on the spectrum from manageable trickster to out-of-control monster.

> If you resist doing what you need (and actually want) to be doing, understand your resistance is not because you're lazy, unmotivated, disorganized, ADHD, or whatever litany of criticisms you've been led to believe is wrong with you. There is nothing wrong with you. The problem is your inner patriarch aka your wounding/wounded or broken masculine function. Its voice may seem to be you. You may believe it is you. It may be driving much of your thinking and action. It is not, however, you. It is an aberration.

The patriarchal masculine wounds us because it is wounded, formed in a sociopathic system that believes doing is more important than being, thinking is a higher function than feeling, and mind is superior to body. These beliefs are deeply embedded in our cultural DNA. This is why we override a gut impulse, going instead with what we *think* we should do. It's why productivity is synonymous with excellence, when sitting still may well be the better use of our time. Why we fall prey to habitual patterns and compulsive action even though deep inside us we'd rather not. Why when asked what we're feeling, we draw a blank. Why so many people are split between the way they act and the way they feel. Why most of us live way more in our heads than in our bodies, thinking, perseverating, projecting, and creating nonstop narratives that are often not connected to reality.

An entrepreneur I know tells a story of hiring someone based on their impressive resume even though he had a bad feeling about them. A year or two in, it was clear he'd made a mistake. The person was disruptive in the workplace and not even good at the job. Termination, however, turned out to be a nightmare. It took an expensive lawsuit and large severance pay to finally separate them from his company. "Ah yes," he said to me, "I should have listened to those feelings."

Human Beings or Human Doings

Take a moment to consider where you are on the spectrum of human being and human doing. The odds are you fall closer to the human doing end. It's ironic we call ourselves "human beings." If only we actually were. The sad truth is that centuries of patriarchal conditioning have left us evolutionarily hardwired to be much more comfortable when we're busy doing something. Even when that something is a big nothing. Even when that something has horrifying consequences. Doing something, doing anything, is better than being still.

Most days, I make a pot of chai, which for the uninitiated is a strong brew of Assam tea in an infusion of freshly grated ginger, cardamom, black peppercorns, and cloves. Sweetened with honey and cut with milk, I drink this throughout the day. In the morning, it's still piping hot. By afternoon it needs reheating. This takes two minutes. You would think that after all my years of meditation practice, I would gratefully sink into this brief moment of pause as I wait for my tea to heat up. But no. I still have to push back against the compulsion to pick up my phone and check email and text messages. It really is pathological.

Human beings would never be so cruel as to rape, plunder, make war, enslave, and in all ways carry on with no thought to the repercussions of their actions. Human beings would never put profit over people, animals, plants, and communities. Human beings would never destroy the planet. Only human doings plow ahead with these insane behaviors. We have got to break the doing compulsion. We have got to make friends with being.

> Boy, I hurried . . . I hurried for a long time.
> I'm sorry I did. All the time you're hurrying,
> you're not really as aware as you should be.
> You're trying to make things happen instead
> of just letting it happen.
> —*Bob Dylan*

> I know the idiot's warehouse
> Is always full.
>
> I know each of us
> Could run back and forth from there
> All day long
>
> And show everyone our vast collection.
> Though tonight, Hafiz,
> Retire from the madness for an hour,
>
> Gather with some loyal friends
> Or sit alone
>
> And
> Sing beautiful songs
>
> To God.
> —*Hafiz/Ladinsky*

The rich industrialist from the North was horrified to find the Southern fisherman lying lazily beside his boat smoking a pipe.

"Why aren't you out fishing?" said the industrialist.

"Because I have caught enough fish for the day," said the fisherman.

"Why don't you catch some more?"

"What would I do with it?"

"You could earn more money," was the reply. "With that you could have a motor fixed to your boat to go into deeper waters and catch more fish. Then you would make enough money to buy nylon nets. These would bring you more fish and more money. Soon you would have enough money to own two boats . . . maybe even a fleet of boats. Then you would be a rich man like me."

"What would I do then?"

"Then," said the industrialist, "you could really enjoy life."

"What do you think I'm doing right now?"

—*Traditional Story*

Growing a Healthy Masculine

Years ago, I spent time at my guru's ashram in India. We were in a small village about three hours from Mumbai. Every day I'd wake before the sun, wash, get dressed, and head over to the main hall for the morning meditation. This was my favorite time of day, that magical window when the sky is dark and stars are visible, but the promise of dawn is in the air. The session ran from 4:30 to 6:00 a.m., so by the time I came outside again, it was light. I'd get a glass of chai and sit under a tree, sipping my tea and enjoying the quiet. Then I'd walk along a garden path to the courtyard for the morning chant. This was my daily ritual. I loved every moment.

Then one morning as I stood up to walk to the courtyard, I was overwhelmed by waves of panic and despair. It was awful. Had I been in the States, I'd have packed my bags, gotten into my car, and driven home. However, I was in a remote village in India. Escape was not an option. I stood there for a moment, trembling with dread, and then the inner voice I later came to recognize as my healthy masculine kicked in, reminding me of other times I'd felt this way, reminding me that every time I had, I'd fled, reminding me that fleeing had never worked, and suggesting that maybe this time, since I had no choice anyway, maybe, just maybe, I could try not fleeing.

I kept walking, talking to myself in this way, taking one step after another, telling myself I could feel this despair and not go back to my room and hide, telling myself I did not have to run away. By the time I got to the courtyard, I was feeling more steady. By the time I sat down, I was feeling okay. And a few minutes later, when the morning chant began, I felt absolutely fine.

This was a life-changing moment. While I didn't yet have the language to explain what had just happened, I knew I'd won an important battle inside myself. My wounding masculine took a powerful hit that day. It would take another decade for my healthy masculine to stabilize, but this was the beginning of the inner patriarch's demise.

A Couple of Writing Prompts for Those Who Like to Journal

1. Remember a time when you pushed through fear, doubt, unworthiness, overwhelm, or boredom. Describe the situation including what you were feeling and what you were hearing in your mind.

2. Make a list of the ways your wounding/wounded masculine distorts your sense of self and a list of the ways your healthy masculine sees you clearly and supports you.

Chapter 3

DISMEMBERMENT AND RECLAMATION

Only by discovering and loving the goddess
lost within our rejected body
can we hear our own authentic voice.
—Marion Woodman

I came of age in the late 1960s and early '70s, during the postwar explosion of second-wave feminism. For the women I knew, the word of that time was "reclamation." Patriarchy had distorted our sense of self, robbing us of healthy relationships with our bodies, hearts, and minds. We were the dismembered daughters of Eve, formed on a whim from Adam's rib, and along with that infamous snake, maligned for millennia for taking a risk for knowledge.

The story of Adam and Eve was the first iconic myth I realized was a lie. Not that I'd believed the literal tale, or for that matter, thought much about it. As I've said before, my parents were atheists, so biblical stories were not part of my nurture. Still, I understood the Bible was key in the development of the Western psyche. So my reading-between-the-lines revelation—that Eve was not the problem, that Eve had never been the problem, and that the serpent's real crime in this patriarchal remake was his prior role as sacred to the goddess—hit me hard. I wondered how much of my own self-doubt went back to that primal story of "Woman" being the reason for the "Fall of Man."

Enter the Great Mother

It was around this time I discovered Erich Neumann's book *The Great Mother*. In that early '70s era, to put these two words—great and mother—together was just not done. Mothers (not to mention all women) were held in low esteem. Any greatness we might have was overlooked and undermined. Sure there'd been standouts over the centuries, but they were exceptions, generally regarded with suspicion. For young women of that time, models of female power were hard to come by.

For me, reading Neumann's work challenged all that. Here was a 400-page book from a revered university press articulating a hidden history of sacred feminine primacy, of great mother iconography, of complex constellations of goddesses who'd been revered for thousands of years. Reading it, I realized the cartoon-like goddesses I knew from Greek and Roman myths were part of a vast tableau of feminine archetypes that, in the patriarchal turning from Great Mother to Father God, had been suppressed, repressed, co-opted, dismembered, and forgotten. And yet the spectrum of feminine power was mighty. The Goddess was a living thread from time immemorial, the light of the soul, the ground of being, yet we were all blind to "her." It was astonishing.

This was the beginning of my reclamation of the essential power I began thinking of as the deep feminine. I began to understand that goddesses were blueprints of something buried inside of us. I didn't yet understand that the feminine had nothing to do with gender, that the feminine was the ground of everyone's being, and that reclamation of the feminine ground would be essential work for the twenty-first century. That insight would come later.

Patriarchy in Drag

As my own journey into the deeper meaning of the goddess continued, I began questioning the focus of the women's movement. I began suspecting that as women moved into the workplace, taking our hard-fought place as equal to men, something vital was left out of the equation: the feminine.

While we made a correct observation—that male supremacy was a serious problem—we embraced an incorrect solution: that we needed to become like men. So we ended up buying into a value system—mind over body, doing over being, ranking over linking, competition over cooperation—that was seriously flawed. It was this flawed system that needed to be addressed. Instead, we now had patriarchy masquerading as women's liberation—a veritable patriarchy in drag—continuing the eons-long project of dismemberment from the feminine ground.

The Murder and Dismemberment of Tiamat

Let me underline the phrase "eons-long." The first story I know of that articulates this split is three to four thousand years old. It's from a Babylonian myth that describes the murder and dismemberment of Tiamat, the Great Goddess, by her nephew Marduk. An important story in the evolution of consciousness, it charts the shift from holistic worldview embodied in metaphors of the Great Mother, to the hierarchical worldview embodied in metaphors of God the Father. In other words, it articulates the beginning of the patriarchal project.

In this story, Tiamat's husband is annoyed with their children, who he claims disturb his sleep. So he decides to kill them. Tiamat warns her oldest son of trouble at home, suggesting he and his siblings disappear until their father calms down. Rather than listen to Mom, however, he decides to kill the old man. When Tiamat realizes her son has murdered her husband, she becomes angry. Terrified of her rage, he and his brother appeal to their cousin Marduk, asking him to challenge Tiamat. They don't think much will come of this. They only want her distracted long enough to forget the betrayal. Alas, things go very differently. Marduk brutally murders and dismembers Tiamat and declares himself king of the gods.

In order to justify this murder, the storytellers portray Tiamat as a raging demoness, ignoring the fact that she has every right to be outraged by her betraying husband and murdering son. Casting Tiamat as an evil demoness, Marduk becomes the hero of the story.

This is a clever plot device, but also a gross distortion of Tiamat's absolutely appropriate rage. I mean really, her son just murdered her husband and colluded against her with his cousin. If that's not just cause, I don't know what is. Tiamat is not the raging demoness portrayed in these texts. Tiamat is the salty sea, the fertile darkness, the sacred wellspring giving birth to the world.

Tiamat's death and dismemberment articulate how the patriarchal mind (in the form of Marduk) cuts itself off from the feminine ground. Tiamat (personified as the watery depths of the Great Mother) is a metaphor for this ground. Marduk personifies the distortion of the masculine impulse to individuate, yes, but not to sever itself from its essential anchoring in the feminine. Tragically, this story goes on day in and day out. From the inner realm within each one of us, to the structures of societies, to the living Earth herself, we are all dismembered in patriarchy.

The mind/body split is a form of dismemberment. Alienation is a form of dismemberment. Addiction is a form of dismemberment. Cruelty is a form of dismemberment. Racism is a form of dismemberment. War is a form of dismemberment. Social policies that cause poverty and homelessness are forms of dismemberment. Human-caused climate change is a form of dismemberment. Pathology is a form of dismemberment. Acting against ourselves is a form of dismemberment. Believing we are powerless is a form of dismemberment.

Remembering Myself

It was fifty years ago, but I remember the moment like yesterday. It was a beautiful summer day. I was lying in the grass soaking up sun when I suddenly became aware that I couldn't feel my belly. It was as if that entire part of my body was dead. This was the early

1970s. We were not yet talking about mind/body awareness, so I had no reference for what I was sensing. Still, there it was, clear as day. It was as if the abdominal region of my body was not there. I could feel my arms and legs. I could feel my chest, shoulders, neck, and head. But the upper and lower thirds of my body seemed split off from the middle.

I put my hands on my belly to see if I might feel something. That's when the flow of memories began. Second-wave feminism notwithstanding, my mother was very critical of her body and therefore very critical of mine. I saw how my young girl's body had been a target of her own self-loathing. She might not have believed in God, but she did believe in counting calories. In her religion, carbohydrates were the enemy and a thousand calories a day was the golden rule.

I remembered being in grade school. All the other kids had peanut butter and jelly sandwiches on white bread and Hostess cupcakes in their lunch boxes. I had to bring a container of tuna salad and eat it with a fork. It was mortifying. I remembered how her frequent critiques of the way I looked filled me with shame.

I didn't yet know about inner work and had never heard the term "solar plexus." I didn't know the belly is a crucial center of power or that our bodies store impressions of everything that's happened to us in our lives. I didn't know the story of Tiamat and would not have used the word "dismemberment" to describe what I was now seeing. But that was the moment I knew I'd been dismembered and needed to figure out how to get my abdominal section reattached. That was the day I realized I had to remember myself.

Chapter 4

THE GREAT REMEMBERING

There is a void felt these days by women and men—
who suspect that their feminine nature, like Persephone, has gone to hell.
The female void [can only] be cured . . .
by an integration of its parts, by a remembering.
—Nor Hall

Dismemberment happens as the mind untethers itself from being. A long, slow process that begins in childhood and continues until we learn to stop it, dismemberment is the favored weapon of the wounding masculine.

I've worked with many people over the years. Everyone comes in various stages of dismemberment. We can't help it. We're formed in a system that relies on this dysfunction to keep it going. Here's the good news. Once we begin to see clearly, we're on the path to remembering ourselves.

Forms of dismemberment

—Addiction
—Cruelty
—War
—Social policies that cause poverty and homelessness
—Human-induced climate change
—Acting against ourselves
—Believing we are powerless

The Awesome Power of the Enough Moment

The Greek myth of Demeter and Persephone offers a map of this path. It tells the story of Demeter, the Goddess of Grain, and her daughter Persephone. In the Greek hierarchy of gods and goddesses, Demeter is one of the twelve Olympians. This places her right near the top. Yet even Demeter is at risk of forgetting who she is. Which is exactly what happens when, on a beautiful summer day, Persephone is abducted by Hades (the Lord of the Underworld, who happens to be her uncle) and disappears without a trace.

Demeter wanders the earth searching for her lost daughter. Consumed by grief, she slowly forgets that she is a divine being, that she is an Olympian no less, that she is a very powerful mother goddess. After many months of wandering, she ends up in the village of Eleusis, where she takes a job as nursemaid to a baby boy. While her conscious mind has forgotten who she is, her body remembers—she is a mother goddess after all and the body never forgets—and the child thrives under her care. Demeter lovingly tends him throughout the day, and at night when the house is quiet, holds him in the ritual fire to make him an immortal.

One evening his mother happens to look in. Seeing her son consumed by flames, she begins to scream. The absurdity of a mortal woman challenging her divine impulse enrages Demeter, and in the clarity of her rage, she remembers herself. She remembers who she is.

Rising to her full goddess stature, her radiance filling the room, she walks through the house, proclaiming, "Enough, I have had enough. I am Demeter."

From this point on, things begin to resolve. Hades and Zeus—it turns out that uncle and father were in collusion—are forced to release Persephone, or Demeter will make the land barren. Since one of her attributes is Goddess of Grain, this is no empty threat. Barren land means the people will starve. Starving people means no offerings to the gods. No offerings to the gods threatens their divine well-being. Needless to say, a deal is cut and Persephone returns.

Yes.

Demeter's "enough moment" is a metaphor for the inner work of remembering ourselves. The story articulates those moments when we see clearly, and suddenly everything shifts. Fear, loss, hurt, pain, and powerlessness lift, and we find ourselves standing strong in the ground of being. Every "enough" moment is a step on the journey of reclamation and coming home.

Clear Seeing and the Power of Rage

The secret of clear seeing turns out to be, as Demeter's story so aptly suggests, connecting with our rage. It's in the upsurge of this potent fire that we begin to know (i.e., remember) who we are. I'm not talking about reactive anger that is actually a toxic discharge of feelings of powerlessness. Far too many of us have been witness to and victim of this kind of behavior. This is not the rage I'm talking about. Reactive anger is a distortion, an expression of profound dismemberment.

Many people I've worked with have this distorted model for anger. When I bring up the topic of rage as a portal into truth and remembering, they look at me as if I've lost my mind. No, your angry father, mother, sibling, teacher, lover, or other is not a model of clean, healthy rage. The rage I'm talking about hurts no one. The rage I'm talking about reestablishes truth in the room.

> I'm not talking about reactive anger that is actually a toxic discharge of feelings of powerlessness. . . . The rage I'm talking about hurts no one. The rage I'm talking about reestablishes truth in the room.

I Have Had Enough

I was twenty-five years old, a young woman and new mother trapped in a loveless marriage to an angry, controlling man. Rather than seeing that the way he treated me was abuse, I did what every victim does. I tried to read his moods and accommodate. The truth was, he enraged and repulsed me. But I was way too wounded to admit this to myself. In those days, I was a master of denying what my feelings were clearly saying.

One evening we were having dinner and the light over the dining table blew out. He had a phobia about electricity, so rather than getting up to change the bulb, he began berating me. This was the pattern of our marriage. Every problem, large or small, was somehow my fault. I'd grown so numb to this, I never pushed back, just did what needed to be done and carried on.

The light that needed to be changed hung from the ceiling but plugged into an outlet underneath the table, so replacing the bulb was a bit of a production. I had to get up from the table to get the stepladder and a new bulb, crawl under the table to unplug the electric cord, crawl back out from under the table to get up on the stepladder so I could unscrew the bad bulb, screw in the good one, and then crawl back under the table to plug in the cord. I did all this, and when the light came on, the LIGHT came on.

My soon-to-be-ex-husband had been standing there the whole time yelling and carrying on, not so different from the irate mother shrieking at Demeter. From my vantage point—I'd just pushed the plug into the outlet so was still under the table—he looked so ridiculous, I started to laugh. In that moment, I saw the absurdity of our marriage. Although I didn't yet have the language to understand what had just happened, I did know that everything had changed. I came out from under the table still laughing, looked him straight in the eye, and said, "Never again."

As often happens when we stand our ground—which is shorthand for standing in the ground of being—things shift (at least temporarily) into a more harmonious place. He had a moment of remorse, and we had a couple of months of relative calm.

The day it all ended started like any other. My sister was visiting and we were out all morning with my two-year-old daughter. We weren't expecting him back until dinner, so I'd not yet done the daily tidying up. For some reason he came home early, and when he saw I hadn't vacuumed, threw one of his tantrums. This was my "enough" moment, the moment when, like Demeter, I remembered who I was. And I was done.

My sister gave me a thumbs-up and took my daughter out of the house. I gave him a you've-got-to-be-kidding-me look, grabbed my handbag, and said I'd given it my all but the marriage was over; that we were going out, that he should pack his bags and find a place to stay. He left the next morning. And me, I stepped full-hearted and full-bellied into my newly emerging, reclaiming, and remembering life.

Interlude

DARK NIGHT OF THE SOUL

The dark night of the soul comes just before revelation.
When everything is lost, and all seems darkness,
then comes the new life.
—Joseph Campbell

One does not become enlightened by imagining figures of light,
but by making the darkness conscious.
—Carl Jung

I tore myself away from the safe comfort
of certainties through my love for truth—
and truth rewarded me.
—Simone de Beauvoir

Chapter 5

OUT OF THE ASHES

There can be no rebirth without a dark night of the soul,
a total annihilation of all that you believed in
and thought that you were.
—Pir Vilayat Khan

The next nine years were a time of great opening as I found my way as a single mother, creative artist, and spiritual seeker. My now ex-husband and I had left New York soon after our daughter was born and were living in a small village in Western Massachusetts. Now that I was raising a child on my own, community and childcare were essential, and I connected with a group of other young parents who wanted to start a co-op preschool. This was rural New England, circa 1973. We were twentysomething, back-to-the land, counterculture folks, urban exiles who'd fled the city in pursuit of pastoral dreams. We set up our school in an old church basement, making everything from scratch and by hand. So weekday mornings, my daughter had a place to go, and apart from my volunteer days, I had several hours to myself.

I'd studied classical music all my life, but after my daughter was born, I was determined to learn how to improvise. This had been a tricky endeavor, because my fortunately now ex-husband had so disparaged my musical life that whenever I sat down at the piano, he would play a Led Zeppelin record at high volume. If I dared ask him to turn it off or down, he'd explode. It was therefore only safe to work on my music during the day when he was out of the house or late at night when he was sleeping. Now, finally, I was free.

Something in me understood that if I wanted to heal, I needed to read every book on Western psychology and Eastern philosophy I could get my hands on, I needed to see a therapist, and I needed to make music that came directly from inside of me, music of my own time and place. It was no longer enough to play music written by European men. I needed to find my own music.

I was twenty years away from realizing that the something in me that understood this was the archetypal field personified as the goddess Saraswatī (more on "her" in Part II), but I was at least beginning to realize that ignoring this voice (which I later came to understand was the voice of my own insight) was generally a bad idea.

I'd written in a journal since I was a young girl, and during my teens began having the experience of shifting into an altered space where the words poured through me. Although I didn't understand how this happened—shout-out to Saraswatī—I liked the way it felt. I liked the sense of opening into a space that seemed bigger than me. I liked the way the words that came had a poetry to them. I liked the sense of wisdom and depth they seemed to carry. I wondered: If I sat at the piano with my hands on the keyboard, maybe even closed my eyes, would something similar happen? When I first tried this, nothing much did. But I kept at it, slowly and tentatively. A few notes here. A melodic line there. A chord progression. A rippling arpeggio. A song without words.

It was during this time that the light began to come. It was so palpable I could see it pouring through my fingers and flowing into the music. Nothing like this had ever happened before, and I'd done my share of psychedelics. This was different. There was no mind-altering substance involved. This light came directly from inside of me. This light was familiar, like it had been around me for a really long time, like it knew me better than I knew myself. And now, it appeared that this light wanted to be known.

I wasn't yet thinking about working with other musicians. I'd been a solo pianist for so long, collaboration was not on my radar. I was also very protective of my musical life. The fact that I no longer had to hide it was still new. So when one of the dads in our preschool—his name was Paul but everyone called him Gaff—heard I was interested in improvisation and invited me to come play with him, I was terrified. Nevertheless, I knew I had to go.

From the moment I stepped into his music room, I was home. Gaff's main instruments were vibraphone and marimba. He also had a huge collection of anything he could coax music from: bells, gongs, chimes, cymbals, whistles, pots, pans, wooden blocks. If he could make it sing, he had it. We sat, we talked, we drank herb tea, and then he took his place at the marimba, beckoned me to the piano, and we started to play. At first he took the lead, showing me how improvisation was just a continuation of our conversation. Only instead of talking in words, we were talking in music. It was all about listening, really listening, and responding to what I heard.

Making music with Gaff was revelatory. It was like we were tossing the light back and forth between us. He showed me I could see the piano as more than purely melodic, that I didn't have to be locked into Western scales and tonality. He handed me a set of mallets one day, urging me to play the strings, to drum on the wooden case, to play the entire instrument. He encouraged me to be fearless, to open my voice and let it go. The most important thing was staying open to whatever was arising inside of me and between us.

Gaff also had an extensive record collection. So along with our music making, he introduced me to African, Indian, and Indonesian music, and to the avant-garde European and American jazz players and composers of our time. He gave me a great gift. Through him, I discovered the music I hadn't known I was looking for, and in that music, I discovered the artist I'd always sensed inside me but hadn't known how to find. In the half century that has now come between us, I've had the good fortune to work with many great musicians. But Gaff is the one who opened the door.

As our collaboration morphed into a collective of dancers and musicians, however, he began pulling back. By then, Sujata, a dancer/choreographer in the group, and I were developing a vision for what later came to be called performance art. In those days, we called it music/dance/theater. We made large- and small-scale works that wove dance, music, memoir, feminism, poetry, and myth. Nowadays, this is par for the course. Back then, it was cutting-edge.

We built a studio and performance space in the town where we lived, and later, as the invitations came, taught and performed in venues in Boston, New York City, and small towns in New England. For years, long after it was all behind us, strangers would stop me on the street and say they'd been at this or that performance and had never forgotten it. It was a passionate, trailblazing decade. It just wasn't sustainable. I was flying too close to the sun and didn't have the grounding I needed to hold me safe in that flight.

Throughout this time I'd also been searching for a spiritual teacher—partly because I wanted to understand what the light was, partly because in that post-hippie era being on an Eastern spiritual path was the thing to do, partly because all the books I was reading on Eastern philosophy were making a strong case for finding a guru, and partly because I sensed this was key to building a more sustainable life for my daughter and me.

I studied with a much-loved Sufi master and sat with three of the great Buddhist monks and teachers of that time. I even tried the lesser-known and somewhat mysterious Gurdjieff Work. But it was all too much heart, too much head, or just didn't feel like home. I wanted a teacher who combined the intellectual rigor of the Work, the openhearted joy of the Sufis, and the sublime presence I felt in the Buddhist masters.

Toward the end of 1977, when I was twenty-nine years old, I found all of that and more on the Hindu yogic path I would travel for the next seventeen years. I loved the way the yogic teachings wove poetry and stories with philosophical dialogue, deconstructing consciousness and the mind with a depth of insight I'd never before encountered. I loved the rituals that were performed in the ashrams, epitomizing the sacred space I'd tried to bring to my own performance work. I loved the stillness of the meditation practice and bliss of the chanting. And the guru himself. I had never experienced a human being with a power like his. And the clincher was, he called that power the shakti. And what was the shakti? The Goddess.

So here I was, this young feminist who'd been studying mythologies of the goddess for close to a decade, loving the stories and imagery, but viewing them as lost to an earlier time. And now, I'd stumbled onto a wisdom path that constellated around a force field considered to be the living goddess. It was, quite simply, amazing.

In the meantime, the relentless demands of teaching, performing, making new work, running a center for the arts, and being a single mother were starting to wear me down. I was exhausted to the bone. So, in 1980, when I was in my early thirties and met and fell in love with the man and fellow devotee I would later marry, I was ready to slow things down and build a simpler life.

Dark Night of the Soul

We spent that summer at our guru's Upstate New York ashram. Toward the end of August, we were invited to stay on and join the winter staff. Our guru would return to India in the fall and we'd be part of the skeleton crew holding down the fort. I'd now been a student of this path for four years. Apart from the decision to not disrupt my daughter's school year, which meant that from September through June she'd live with her father, this invitation was a dream come true.

Several months into my new life, however, the bottom fell out. I was serving the guru whose work I believed would heal the world, living what I thought was my ideal lifestyle, married to the man I thought was the love of my life, and I was miserable.

Before this, my daughter and I had always thrived in my guru's ashrams. So whenever we could get away—weekends, school breaks, summer vacation—that was where we went. Now, this sanctuary had become purgatory. It was all I could do to drag myself to the meditation hall in the morning and do whatever work I had to do throughout the day. All joy, all sense of meaning and purpose, all contentment and luminosity had gone out of my life.

I'd certainly been through my share of hard times. Yet I'd never experienced anything like this. One especially difficult night I was lost in despair, curled up on the floor rocking. My husband coaxed me into bed, suggesting I think about writing a letter to our guru, and I fell asleep whispering, "Help me."

Coming Home

The next morning, I found a brown paper bag with my name on it sitting outside our door. Inside the bag was a music box shaped like a piano. The song it played was "Raindrops Keep Falling on My Head." Holding it in my hand, listening to its music, I had a moment of remembering myself. It was just a moment, but enough to poke a hole in the dark night I was lost inside of.

Later that day, a friend gave me a cassette recording of Schubert's Piano Sonata in B-flat Major. At that point, I'd been living away from my piano for close to a year. Listening to this music, I felt a deep stirring inside me. It was like the piano was calling me home.

And then, at dinner that night, a woman I didn't know approached me in the dining hall, saying she'd heard I played the piano and wondered if I might teach her son. That was when the light broke through. In that moment, I knew it was time to leave the ashram and return to my life in music. This time, though, not only as a composer and performer. This time, teaching music to children.

Prior to this, my only teaching experience had been offering workshops to adults. I had no pedagogical training. What I did have was my life as a creative artist, musician, and mother; a background in classical and improvisational music and theater; my training in yoga and spiritual practice; my study of transpersonal psychology and healing; and now, this mysterious messenger in the form of a music box.

Spring came. We moved to a small town in southern New England, halfway between where we'd lived in Massachusetts and the ashram in Upstate New York. When the school year ended, my daughter joined us. Once she was settled, I began offering piano lessons. My practice grew exponentially. From four students the first year to eight the second to sixteen the third and to more than there were hours for by the fourth. At first I thought I would just be teaching piano. As I gave myself over to the work, however, I discovered there was much more at stake. I was a partner in a sacred trust, charged with carefully tending the creative spark in each student.

I understood I modeled a way of being that my students felt drawn to, something in themselves they recognized in me. There was something about our hour of focused time together, something about my meeting them wherever they might be. A subtle alchemy occurred. I began to see that teaching was so much more than a transfer of information. Teaching was about listening.

Listening, Kinship, and Witnessing

Over the years I saw that the best thing I could do for my students was to meet them where they were, see them as they were, believe in them without condition, and encourage them to laugh. While the piano was a wonderful meeting place, it sometimes got in the way. In my early days of teaching I tiptoed around this, integrating creative arts and guided meditations into the piano lesson. Toward the end of the decade, I began wondering if my work was less about teaching piano and more about teaching life.

Deena was one of the first adults I worked with. I'd taught her daughter through middle and high school, and now that she was going off to college, Deena wanted to study piano with me. When she came for her first lesson, however, rather than sitting at the piano, she sat in the chair at my desk. The next thing I knew she was weeping. Through her tears she told me she'd been seeing a psychiatrist for years, but it just wasn't working. She sensed I knew something other people did not. Whatever it was, she wanted it. That was the day my practice opened from teaching piano to young people to doing inner work with adults.

During those years I earned a master's degree in Expressive Arts Therapy and developed Eyes-Closed Work, the meditation-based modality I still use today. I wasn't yet thinking about the patriarchal structures of consciousness, of "doing" as of the masculine and "being" as of the feminine. I wasn't yet looking at the toxic imbalance of masculine doing over feminine being. These ideas were just beginning to form. What I did know was that the outward gaze of our postmodern age was a serious problem and that the medicine for healing was learning how to turn that gaze within and listen.

Part II

AND THE GODDESS IS THE REMEDY

The spirit of the fountain never dies.
It is called the Mysterious Feminine.
Frail, frail it is, hardly existing,
but touch it, it will never run dry.
—Tao Te Ching

I can't read, but I can hear. I have heard the Bible and have learned that Eve caused man to sin. Well, if woman upset the world, do give her a chance to set it right.
—Sojourner Truth

People lock onto motherhood as a key to feminine identity, in part from the belief that children are the best way to fulfill your capacity to love . . . But there are . . . so many things that need love, so much other work love has to do in the world.
—Rebecca Solnit

There just comes a point when you have to risk becoming more open to the vulnerable side, which I think is the female side. It's much more courageous than the male side.
—Sam Shepard

Chapter 6

THE IMPECCABLE SPLENDOR

In 1989, soon after my forty-first birthday, I had an extraordinary vision in a dream. I'd been reading about the Native American Medicine Wheel, fascinated by the Lakota practice of vision quests and medicine shields. My reading, though, was wholly recreational. I was totally committed to the guru path I'd walked for twelve years. I assumed I'd walk this path to the end of my life.

And then the vision came:

Early evening sky, stars just beginning to appear, no visible moon, and a slow-spinning wheel of light moving toward me. As it came closer, I could see words and images inscribed in the four quadrants of the wheel. I couldn't read the words or discern the images. Nevertheless, in that dream-knowing kind of way, I knew they were important. I could also hear music pouring out from the four cardinal gates. It sounded so beautiful I nearly wept. And I understood—at this point it was as if the vision was speaking to me—that what I was hearing were four musical medicine shields and that they belonged to me. I had a moment of arguing with the vision, explaining there was no such thing as musical medicine shields, and even if there was, this was not my path. I lost that argument pretty quickly. The next thing I knew, the vision drew me into its center, where a group of Sanskrit letters shimmered in a luminous blue sea. And then there was only light.

There are dreams and there are dreams. This was a big one. As to why it had come or what I was supposed to do with it, I had no idea. The only thing I knew was that the vision was a map of some sort, and that I had to find my way back inside it, that I had to find its meaning and its music, and that I had to follow it wherever it led.

Dream Shield Journey

The ensuing journey unfolded over the next nine years. I often had the sense that I was following my nose—that as long as I let the vision guide me, following my instincts no matter how counterintuitive they might seem, sooner or later it would all come clear. My job was to keep listening. And listen I did, every spare moment, writing, painting, walking, dreaming, meditating, and playing the piano.

For the first six years, I assumed the vision was a gift from my guru that would bring me closer to him. As I made my way through what unfolded as four distinct inner journeys, however, rather than meeting my guru, four different aspects of the goddess—Kālī, Lakṣmī, Saraswatī, and Kuan Yin—broke open inside me, each one holding the key to a musical shield.

It wasn't until the end of those six years, however, when I was catapulted out of my then seventeen years' devotion to the guru, that I realized I'd had it all wrong. The vision was not a gift from the guru. The vision was not about bringing me closer to him. The vision was a gift from my own inner being. The vision was about bringing me closer to me.

I will tell you more of that story in the Kuan Yin chapter. For now, it's enough to say that in those final moments of that final journey, I walked on from nearly two decades on the guru path, turning the corner on what had been a long, deep, essential, and now quite unexpectedly over-and-done-with period of my life.

During the last three years of this quest, I recorded the album *Dream Shield Journey* and began offering workshops that constellated around the four goddesses as I now understood them: Kālī, Lakṣmī, Saraswatī, and Kuan Yin. At the end of that period, I taught two daylong Kuan Yin workshops, the first one in Toronto, the second at my yoga-center base in Princeton.

Registration for the Princeton program was so low, I considered canceling. But a very insistent inner voice said it didn't matter how many people were there, I had to teach this workshop. As it turned out, we had excellent turnout and the workshop was sublime. Then, that night, as I climbed into bed, I heard the inner voice again, this time saying, "Soon you will move through the final gate." I had no idea what it was talking about. However, since it was the same voice that told me to teach the workshop regardless of registration numbers—and for that matter, the same voice I'd been losing arguments with since I first told the vision there was no such thing as musical shields—I took it at its word and fell asleep.

The next evening, during my weekly meditation class, I walked through that final gate. I won't tell you the details of that experience. Some things should not be spoken. I will tell you that it was like a cosmic seal of approval, and that it filled me with a profound sense of responsibility to the ever-deepening insight and archetypes of the vision. This was nine long years after it first came. It was only later that I realized the first six had been a training by the vision, the final three, an apprenticeship to it, and that I'd somehow passed its tests.

Writing now, twenty-five years later, I realize that this is yet another gate, and more important, that there is no final gate. There is only staying open, curious, and listening. Always listening.

> There is no final gate. There is only staying open, curious, and listening. Always listening.

The Impeccable Splendor

This book is dedicated to Michael Brooks, a young man I had the good fortune to grow close to during the last four years of his too-short life. Michael was a rare soul. His intellectual genius and comedic gifts were held in a heart so huge it reached out to embrace the entire world.

A brilliant public intellectual with an international following, he was also deeply human. In his death he's been somewhat sainted. Michael would not have liked that. Well, perhaps for a moment he would. Then he'd crack a joke and get over himself. Michael was proud of his humanity, proud of his battle scars, proud of his wounded heart.

Michael often told me he wanted to be impeccable. He used that word a lot. "Impeccable," he would say, "I want to be impeccable in every area of my life. Teach me how to be impeccable." During what turned out to be the last months of our time together, after an Eyes-Closed session, he'd have a look of wonder about him and tell me of the splendor he'd just experienced. I would laugh and say, "Michael, this splendor is what you are. This splendor will teach you all the impeccability you long for. Just keep opening into that, Michael—just keep opening into that."

That splendor was his birthright. It is also yours and mine and everyone's. Even the people we dislike and disapprove of, it is theirs too. It does get covered over. In far too many people it's shrouded in a cement-like veil. Yet it never leaves us, never forgets us, never gives up on us. Years may pass. Lifetimes. And the splendor remains. The impeccable splendor. It is the luminous ground of the ground. Embodying its light is the greatest gift we can give to the world. And the ways of the Goddess are entryways into that light.

Chapter 7

FINDING OUR WAY HOME

Between the conscious and the unconscious, the mind has put up a swing:
all earth creatures, even the supernovas, sway between these two trees,
and it never winds down.
Angels, animals, humans, insects by the million,
also the wheeling sun and moon;
ages go by, and it goes on.
Everything is swinging: heaven, earth, water, fire,
and the secret one slowly growing a body.
Kabir saw that for fifteen seconds, and it made him a servant for life.
—Kabir/Bly

We think we are our bodies and our minds. But we are so much more. We're this huge shimmering awareness, waiting to be remembered and integrated into our sense of self. This integration is the secret of true healing. If you want to transform the patriarchal structures that muck around inside you, contracting everything you are into everything you're not, and making a big mess in the process, I offer you the Goddess.

Now let me be real here. The goddess is a metaphor for the luminous ground of everything we are. Full disclosure: We don't have to personify it as goddess. We don't have to personify it as anything. The truth is, it simply is. To give it name and form is to reduce it. The human mind, however, likes concepts. As far as concepts go, the goddess is an excellent one. Especially for those of us who prefer love, compassion, truth, integrity, and justice to cruelty, domination, delusion, deception, and control.

Meeting the Goddess When We Least Expect It

Elaine came to see me for Eyes-Closed Work soon after her fiftieth birthday. She told me she'd been dealing with depression and anxiety for much of her adult life, yet no matter what treatment was prescribed, nothing seemed to work. She might have a few good months, but sooner or later, the dread would return. She was nervous about Eyes-Closed Work, convinced she'd not be able to do it, and recited the litany I often hear: *I can't meditate, I'm not spiritual, I'm not creative, I don't have an imagination, I'm afraid I'll fail.*

She was, however, desperate enough to try. I assured her there was no right or wrong; that even if nothing seemed to happen, we could work with that; that I'd be with her every step of the way. This seemed to calm her. She lay down on the couch in my office, closed her eyes, and let me guide her into a gentle meditative state.

Within a few moments she began telling me what she was experiencing. "I see myself with ropes wrapped around my hands and attached to my sides," she said. "Big ropes like the ones they use to tie up boats. I'm all alone in my room and can't move."

I asked her how this felt. "Awful," she said. "It's how I feel every morning when I wake up and have to face the day." I suggested she allow herself to feel this discomfort and then if it didn't seem too strange, to try asking the space inside her for help. She took this in and became very quiet. We sat in the silence together.

When it felt to me like something inside her had shifted, I asked what had just happened. She told me that as soon as she asked for help, the walls of the room she'd been alone in disappeared and she saw mountains in the distance. Then her daughter was there. Seeing Elaine unable to free herself, her daughter laughed and said, "That's easy, Mom!" as she gently untied the ropes.

Still deep in the vision space of Eyes-Closed Work, Elaine told me that now that her hands were unbound, she didn't know what to do with them. I suggested she ask them directly. To her amazement, her hands said they wanted her to fly. The next thing Elaine knew, a winged horse appeared. She climbed onto its back, and they flew off together. Initially she said she was having "a nice feeling of sailing over the hills and looking down." Then suddenly, she was back in the room with a feeling of heaviness. "Heaviness is sort of a habit," she said sadly. "I feel myself looking out with a sense of hopelessness, a sick feeling in my stomach. It's despair. I guess flying is just not for me."

I encouraged her to stay with the sense of heaviness and despair and see what, if anything, might happen. After a few minutes, she began having images again. "I'm looking at the green hills and the bluish-purple mountains off in the distance. There's a woman standing there. All in purple. She's very tall, dressed in a long cloak, and carrying a walking stick. She's beckoning me to come, to walk with her. As her stick hits the air it makes sparks. She swings it exuberantly. Full of energy. She swings it all around me. It's very nice. She gives me the stick as a gift, so that I can create my own energy. She says she will be my friend. She tells me her name and says all I have to do is think of her. She is very generous."

"Not bad," I told her, "for someone who didn't think she could do Eyes-Closed Work!" We had a good laugh over that.

Elaine and I continued working together over the next several months, unpacking the imagery from her journey and giving her tools for bringing the meaning, message, and direct experience of the goddess into her daily life. At her final session I was struck by how different she was from the woman who first showed up at my door. "You look so beautiful," I told her, "wide open, luminous, and dare I say it, happy!"

Taking my hands into hers, she smiled so sweetly and said, "Thank you for showing me the way home."

We Meet the Goddess in Myriad Ways

We meet the goddess in myriad ways. With every flash of insight and inspiration, in the wisdom that channels through our mind, in the oneness we feel in nature, in the joy of love and agony of loss. We feel it in the depth and power of our own presence, in the glory of a beautiful day, in the wonder of being alive, in the recognition of the interconnectedness of all life, in the stillness of death. It is always here.

It is at once unknowable, ineffable, and the most familiar presence we have ever known. And this impeccably splendid luminous ground, this fearless pulsation of truth and determination, of magnificence and wonder, of insight and inspiration, of compassion and love—all of this sits right inside us and is always calling us home.

When I was a little girl, I was terrified of being separated from my mother. I was afraid to play at friends' houses, nervous when I had to stay with babysitters, and my mom had to walk me to and from kindergarten every day. These were very different times from now. This was 1954. Back then kids walked to school. I don't remember even having school buses. For that matter, no car seats or seat belts, no bicycle helmets, no backpacks for our books, and no down jackets to keep us warm in the cold snowy winters.

We lived about a mile from my elementary school, which was at the bottom of a long hill. I think my mom was hoping I'd be willing to walk with friends when I started first grade. But I had what today we call severe separation anxiety, and there was no way I was going anywhere without her. I think she was so concerned about me, and also desperate for her own autonomy, that although in those days play therapy was very rare, she somehow found a child therapist and took me to see her each week. I loved going there. There was a magical feeling to the place. I called it the fairy-tale house. The woman who worked with me was very kind. We played together, drew pictures, and talked. I always felt safe with her. Years later I realized that while I'd been having my session downstairs, my mom was upstairs having hers.

At first, nothing changed. My mom and I walked to school and back every day. Once a week we went to the fairy-tale house. Then one day when I came out of school, she wasn't there. I had a momentary panic, then saw her waving from a hundred feet away. When I reached her she hugged me, saying what a brave girl I was, and we walked the rest of the way home. Needless to say, this was the plan she'd been working on in her therapy. The next morning she congratulated me for walking that stretch by myself and said that today she'd drop me off and meet me at that same spot. And so it went. Day by day she increased our distance in tiny steps, always careful to leave me off and wait for me where I could see her.

There were two major stopping places on the hill, the first about a third of the way up, the second about two-thirds of the way. At the top of the hill, you had to cross a street, then walk another long block to get to our house. When she dropped me off one morning, she suggested we meet at the first stopping place. Although I'd not be able to see her until I'd made it halfway there, I was willing to give it a try.

I still remember the thrill of walking what was just a short half block on my own, then seeing her in the distance and running the rest of the way. A week or two later she suggested we meet at the second stopping place. And a week or two after that, at the top of the hill. I don't think it ever occurred to me that I was now walking most of the way to school and home by myself. I always had the sense that she was with me, that I was tethered to her, and that I was safe.

Then came the day I expected her to be at the top of the hill. When I got there, however, she wasn't there. I looked both ways and crossed the street, thinking I'd see her now. Still, no waiting mom. At this point I began feeling annoyed and walked the final block to our house, my six-year-old's indignation growing. I went stomping into the house and angrily confronted her, saying, "Where were you?" I think we can say this was my first Demeter "enough" moment. And there she was with a big grin on her face, saying, "You did it!" And there I was, suddenly realizing I had, feeling utter and absolute joy.

After that I became a walker. After that I was no longer afraid to be alone. These are great gifts my mother gave me. I suspect the level of patience and nurture required to hold me in this process did not come easily to her. And yet she held the space until I could walk on my own. She showed me I could do what scared me. She showed me that even if I couldn't always see it, that I was always held. She showed me that I would always find my way home.

The Goddess *Is* Your Very Best Friend

In the pages that follow, we'll unpack four archetypes of the goddess: Kālī, Lakṣmī, and Saraswatī, who come down through the Hindu tradition, and Kuan Yin, who comes down through Chinese Buddhism. In actuality, these archetypes transcend time, place, geography, cultural construct, and gender. They also transcend the patriarchal traditions that claim them as their own.

As you read on, please allow your analytical and literal, not to mention patriarchal, mind to relax. I'll tell you more stories from my life and from the lives of people I've known. I'll also tell you creation myths of Kālī, Lakṣmī, Saraswatī, and Kuan Yin. You'll find tidbits of yogic philosophy and psychology, and commentary, musings, poetry, mantras, and a handful of inner work practices you can do.

Please remember that the goddess is more experiential than intellectual, more spiraling circles than direct line, more metaphor and impression than stone-cold fact. I strongly suggest you read all this as if you are stepping into an abstract painting or listening to a piece of music; that you read it with your heart as well as your mind. While you might want to understand and connect every dot, it is so much more important to feel yourself in these pages. And to rest in that.

When we venture into the spaciousness of our inner being, we come into a realm that is not ordered in the ways we're used to ordering. It often doesn't make sense, in the ways we think we know what sense is. As I've reiterated so many times in this writing, the ground of being simply is. It also has a wicked sense of humor. It's been laughing at my feeble attempts to doubt, resist, challenge, and control it for much of my adult life. I suspect that as you get to know it better, you'll hear it laughing at you too.

The realm of being is terrifying to the patriarch. This is why Marduk has to murder and dismember Tiamat. He simply cannot tolerate what he experiences as darkness and chaos, and what is actually the sublime unknowable everythingness of being. This is why Zeus and Hades have to abduct Persephone. They can't tolerate the joyous aliveness embodied in the feminine whole. They have to try to break it up. I think they feel it laughing at them, even as they attempt to destroy it. I think it's the goddess's laughter that sends them over the edge.

We need never fear the realm of being. Especially when we can delight in its laughter, rest in its darkness, open into its light. Especially since the realm of being, not Marduk or Zeus or Hades or our own patriarchal masculine, holds the truth of what we are. This truth has been holding us from the beginning of time. We may turn away from it, we may think it is not here, we may think we know better, we may think the whole notion is a sham—until that day we hear it laughing and dissolve into its enormous embrace.

Chapter 8

MAPS FOR THE JOURNEY

A Note About Sanskrit Grammar and Transliteration

Writing Sanskrit words within English-language conventions can be confusing. For example, Sanskrit does not use capital letters. Every word is spelled in what we call "lowercase." With Sanskrit words that have found their way into the English language, however, I tend to go with English-language conventions. So if I'm writing words like "Sanskrit" or "Kālī," which are proper names, I capitalize them. Along these same lines, if I'm writing words like "dharma" or "yoga," and they're the first word of a sentence, I capitalize them too.

Then there's the question of transliteration. I prefer using transliterated spellings of Sanskrit words because I see this as more respectful of the tradition. However, I want this book to be as reader-friendly as possible. So I'm splitting the difference. Deity names and mantras are keeping their transliterated spelling. With words like "chakra," however, rather than going with the transliterated "cakra" spelling, I'm using the English "chakra." And when I use a Sanskrit word or phrase that has not found its way into common English usage, I italicize it.

Here's a guide to transliterated Sanskrit pronunciation.

Vowels

a as in "but" or "cup"
ā as in "calm" or "father"
i as in "bit" or "sit"
ī as in "seen" or "mean"
u as in "put" or "foot"
ū as in "room" or "mood"
ṛ pronounced like a rolled r with a short u sound following it
ai as in "aisle"
au as in "bough" or "now"

Consonants

c as in "such"
jñ as in "nya"
ś slight whistle as in "shawl"
ṣ similar to ś with slightly less whistle/duration, as in "shun"
ḥ at the end of a phrase indicates the previous vowel is echoed; e.g., "aha"

A Note About the Goddess Mantras Featured in This Book

The simplest way to understand mantras is to think of them as proper names. In fact, the yogic tradition refers to chanting mantras as "singing the name." Naming is powerful. If you call my name, I respond. Just hearing the sound of my name is enough to get my attention, as is the quality or energy of that sound. If your voice sounds friendly, I respond in kind. If your voice sounds harsh or angry, I'm less open to talking to you. And while it's true that calling my name gets my attention, it's the actual energy of your voice that makes the difference between holding or losing my attention. It's the energy of our voice that makes the impact. We may forget every word a person said. What we remember is how we felt talking with them.

The goddess mantras featured in this book are not so different. Rather than people, though, they name specific energy fields, aka archetypes, embedded in our psyches. These are energetic patterns, akin to blueprints or algorithms, that articulate the very best within us. When we work with these mantras, we're singing the names of these archetypal fields.

And here's where it gets interesting. The mantras are considered sonic forms of these fields. It's like the archetype is an energetic shape and the mantra is the sound of that shape. There's tremendous resonance between them. Energy fusing with energy. Like a sound and light show, the archetype draws the mantra to it and the mantra shapes, refines, and strengthens the archetype.

This is heady stuff so take it in as best you can. If you remember nothing else, remember this: When we move into the realm of mantra, we're moving into the realm of sound and vibration. We're less interested in materiality, physical form, or meaning. We're after deep experiential opening and expansion of consciousness.

The Sanskrit language places more emphasis on the sound of a word than on what the word stands for. For those of us raised in meaning-based languages like English, this is a tough concept to grasp. We want to understand everything. Sorry. Mantras transcend our understanding. Sanskrit is a language of the heart. The mind may not comprehend it, but the heart will open and receive it. We need not understand a mantra to reap tremendous benefit from working with it.

The Mantras

In the next four chapters, you'll meet Kālī, Lakṣmī, Saraswatī, and Kuan Yin, along with a core mantra for each one. Here they are in transliterated Sanskrit:

om śrī kālī mā

om śrī lakṣmī mā

om śrī saraswatī mā

om śrī kuan yin mā

You can see that they're built from the same base—om śrī ____ mā—with the name inserted within the longer mantra. If we were in class now, and you asked what these mantras mean, I'd give you the lecture about Sanskrit being more about sonic vibration than meaning, and remind you that even repeating them silently will give you more bang for your buck than trying to understand them. But we're here on the pages of this book, and I'd like to make mantra as accessible as possible. So here's a bit of unpacking that will hopefully satisfy the need for meaning.

Om is considered the sound from which the entire universe is created. This is not so different from the New Testament's "In the beginning was the Word . . ." This is why every mantra begins with "om."

Śrī is a term of endearment. Think of it as saying "dear one." Since these mantras are calling us into ourselves, using the śrī endearment is an act of offering love to oneself. Śrī is also translated as "sweet." So you can think of your love offering as a sweet one.

Mā refers to the feminine ground of being. Mā is where we land. So in this mantric formulation, om opens us into the power of the mantra, śrī sweetens its force with love, the name evokes the innate energy of the mantra, and mā is the ground on which we stand.

As we repeat a mantra, either silently or out loud, the energy of that mantra moves into our mind/body system, seeking and energizing its corresponding archetypal field. For example, the mantra *om śrī kālī mā* is singing the name of Kālī. You'll learn more about "her" in the next chapter. For now, think of Kālī as the force or power—the Sanskrit term is "shakti"—of truth. And not just any truth. Kālī is the force of truth that protects innocence and wisdom. When we call its name, the force of its archetypal field responds. So that working with *om śrī kālī mā* fosters connection to our innate sense of truth and authenticity, feeding qualities like clarity, courage, determination, and fierce, protecting love.

Like everything in life, mantras need to be well used and cared for. The more we work with them, cherishing, respecting, and just plain loving them, the more they give back to us.

A Very Short Guide to Hindu Mythology

Hindu mythology has a complex hierarchy of divine beings. You'll encounter a handful of them in the creation stories coming in the next few chapters. Here's a basic primer.

At the very top of the hierarchy is the supreme trinity—the Sanskrit term is "trimūrti"—of Brahma, Viṣnu, and Śiva, personifications of the cosmic functions of creation, sustaining, and transformation. Although in the traditional (aka patriarchal) formulation, the sacred feminine gets second-class billing, each of the supreme three has a goddess half: Brahma and Saraswatī, Viṣnu and Lakṣmī, and Śiva and Kālī. Sitting below them, in various categorical rankings, are the demigods and demigoddesses, along with a full spectrum of divine beings, from the most sublime to the most demonic.

Mythological stories are best read as mirrors. The more we step inside them, seeing ourselves in every character and detail, the more insight we glean about ourselves and the world.

> When you step further into the story, not only does the mythic territory open, but the deep self moves and the world of imagination and meaning comes toward you.
>
> —*Michael Meade*

Chapter 9

KĀLĪ

How can you help
but grow wise
with such teachings
as these—
the untrimmable light
of the world,
the ocean's shine,
the prayers that are made
out of grass?
—Mary Oliver

Hindu cosmology divides time into four ages that are called yugas. Scholars disagree about how long each yuga lasts (bottom line: thousands of years), and therefore, about which yuga we're currently in. Looking at the empirical evidence, I think it's fair to say we're deep in Kālī Yuga. Listen to this description from *Srimad Bhagavatam*, an ancient Hindu text:

> *Day after day righteousness will decline; wealth alone will be the criterion for worth of character. Strength alone will determine who is just. Even the administration of justice will be perverted by bribery and corruption. Hairstyles will determine beauty. Vehemence of speech will determine truth. People will be overtaken by famine, pestilence, drought and storms, their wealth drained by taxation and robbery, and their energy depleted. Even trees will become stunted on account of their ruthless exploitation by unrighteous men.*

How's that for a poetic description of the time in which we live? Welcome to Kālī Yuga. The text goes on to say that "there is one great redeeming feature in Kālī Yuga: that one can reach the Supreme by merely singing the names of the divine." Now, I'm a big fan of the benefits of chanting, so have always loved this idea. As the goddess Kālī came alive for me, however, I began sensing a deeper connection between Kālī and Kālī Yuga. And perhaps a more interesting one: Kālī brings the patriarch to its knees.

Think of a mother bear protecting her young. This is the energy of Kālī. Kālī lives within us as the courage to stand strong in the face of battle and the neutralizer of that which causes harm, as the sword of discrimination and the wisdom to know where to place the blade. Kālī embodies the warrior archetype, blazing in the clarity of the "enough" moment. When Kālī takes its rightful place inside us, the masculine finds its proper shape inside us and becomes what it is meant to be: a vehicle for truth, justice, compassion, and love in the world.

Kālī to the Rescue

Paul comes in for a session, nervous about a competitive coworker he suspects is vying for his position in the company. We talk about his lifelong pattern of keeping a low profile so as not to bring attention to himself, then resenting people who get the attention he craves. We shift into Eyes-Closed Work. After a few minutes he sees an image of his boychild self seething with anger, but unable to speak.

Sitting with this image opens a flood of memories. He talks about growing up in a chaotic home, of learning to stay quiet to make himself invisible, of becoming the dutiful child who never rocks the boat. We sit quietly together, giving him space to remember and to feel.

I suggest he work with the mantra *om srī kālī mā*, repeating it silently and imagining it like a shield around his boychild self. When he opens his eyes, he tells me how at first his boychild self was filled with fear. As he recited the mantra, however, the fear morphed into rage. The next thing he knew, he became a white-hot fury intent on destroying everyone who'd ever hurt him. As the fury subsided, he watched his boychild self merge into the man he is today.

At this point in the telling, Paul grew very quiet as tears welled in his eyes. When he could speak again, he told me he'd seen himself holding a chalice filled with a liquid made of shimmering rubies. He realized this liquid was his fury and that he had to drink it. With each sip, he felt himself growing stronger, the upset he began with transforming into Kālī's calling card: fierce determination.

Paul called a week later to tell me everything had changed. The wonder was that he didn't have to do anything. He simply went back to work feeling that Kālīesque presence inside of himself. In this stance, he exuded the combination of calming authority, welcoming presence, and fierce determination that tends to draw good things to us. The next thing he knew, his boss gave him a new assignment, a move that shifted the coworker out of his immediate space. A month later, the troubling dynamic between them had dissolved and she no longer posed a threat.

om srī kālī mā

A Brief Primer on Yogic Psychology

In yogic psychology, we talk about right identification, when we know who and what we truly are (yogis call this the Self) and wrong identification, when we buy into the Debbie Downer narratives the patriarchal masculine loves to spin. These are generally thought patterns that begin with "I am" and go downhill from there. Sometimes they're conscious, sometimes not, but the message is always the same: *I'm a loser. I'm a fraud. I'm weak, stupid, ugly, unworthy, powerless*, etc. The list goes on and on.

I've worked with many people, some who come to me depressed and demoralized, some so miserable that they've come close to ending their lives. As we parse out the threads of their stories, we always find the patriarchal masculine sitting smug and righteous in the mind, running its toxic message-generating machine, weaponizing our emotions and psychological wounds against us, and seducing us into wrong identification with its voice. We really do need to bust up all identification with its presence in our mind/body system.

I first heard the term "right identification" when I came onto the yogic path. The notion that I was not my mind (or my body), that I was something much deeper and more profound, quite literally blew my mind. Forty years later, its veracity still rings true. From the yogic perspective, what we are is the Self. And the Self is yet another name for the ground of being.

The yogic texts define the Self as being of the nature of *satchitananda*, a Sanskrit term that blends three aspects of being into one long word: *sat* is truth, *chit* is consciousness, and *ananda* is bliss. What the texts are saying is that when we experience the spaciousness of being, when we feel completely alive within ourselves, completely at one with everything that is, we're experiencing the yogic ideal of union with the Self—otherwise known as right identification.

Think of Demeter remembering who she actually is. This is right identification. Think of Paul embodying his Kālīesque presence. This is right identification. Think of Elaine, wide open and joyous as we said our goodbyes. This is right identification. Think of me, a young girl terrified to walk home alone, joyously realizing I had actually done it. This is right identification.

Identification with the Self should never be confused with the righteous stance of zealotry or bigotry, with the delusional certainty we experience in people who believe they are right about whatever they are believing in. Anyone who thinks they have a mandate given by God—or whatever—to separate, divide, or cause harm is about as far from the Self as humanly possible. This is simply a grandiose patriarchal masculine, masquerading as the word of God.

> Identification with the Self should never be confused with the righteous stance of zealotry or bigotry, with the delusional certainty we experience in people who believe they are right about whatever they are believing in. Anyone who thinks they have a mandate given by God—or whatever—to separate, divide, or cause harm is about as far from the Self as humanly possible. This is simply a grandiose patriarchal masculine, masquerading as the word of God.

Kālī on the Battlefield

One of the most famous stories of Kālī is told in a Hindu text called *Devī Mahatmyam*, The Glory of the Goddess. This is a text that's been read, chanted, and commented upon for hundreds of years, so there are many versions of this story. Here's a synopsis of my favorite.

It begins, as these stories often do, with a war between the gods and demons. The demons fighting in this particular war have a superpower that makes them invincible. Almost. They can only be killed by a woman. Once the gods discover this—some hundred years into the fighting—they realize they had better call on the Goddess. Initially she comes in the form of Durgā, who, while less fearsome than Kālī, demolishes much of the demon army.

Toward the end of the battle, however, the demons pull a superpower fast one, where each fresh drop of demon blood becomes another demon. At this point Durgā responds with her ultimate superpower, Kālī, who, leaping from the brow of Durgā, annihilates what's left of the demon army. This is Kālī's famous dance of destruction. The warrior goddess, the embodiment of righteous fury, destroying all that causes harm, restoring balance, restoring justice, restoring order.

At this point, traditional versions of the story will tell you that Lord Śiva, concerned that Kālī is out of control, takes the form of a crying infant and lies down in her path. Now let me be clear here. Kālī is driven by compassion and wisdom. Kālī never loses control. Personally I think Śiva's just tired and wants to go home. Take your pick.

Regardless, Śiva knows how to get Kālī's attention. Hearing the cries of innocence, she stops right there and, sitting down among the detritus of a one-hundred-year war, lifts the child to her breast, nursing him until his crying stops.

How's that for a sublime image of perfect integration. The warrior goddess has just saved the world from demon takeover and, without skipping a beat, shifts from fearsome destroyer to loving nurturer.

Yes.

This is an archetypal field we want to embody. She sets the now sated child back on the ground and watches Śiva resume his form (as if she didn't know it was him all along), then nodding to the thousands watching the spectacle, silently withdraws back into the body of Durgā.

om srī kālī mā

Peer into the imagery of this story and we see human history played out from time immemorial. Today we see it most acutely in the horrifying combination of endless wars and climate catastrophe, all brought to us courtesy of the patriarchal (aka demon) mentality that is split off from its own humanity. Integrated humans (and gods) do not make war on one another or on planet Earth. We make peace. We make conversation. We make relationship. We make kinship. Kinship, not kingship.

> Peer into the imagery of this story and we see human history played out from time immemorial. Today we see it most acutely in the horrifying combination of endless wars and climate catastrophe, all brought to us courtesy of the patriarchal (aka demon) mentality that is split off from its own humanity. Integrated humans (and gods) do not make war on one another or on planet Earth. We make peace. We make conversation. We make relationship. We make kinship. Kinship, not kingship.

I Have Had Enough Redux

I was on retreat in the ashram one summer, staying in a women's dorm. The room was small and dark with three bunk beds crammed into it. There was a vestibule for the sink and vanity between the sleeping area and bathroom, so washing up, putting on makeup, and blow-drying our hair was all done in the open. We were a quiet, self-contained group, however, and even with this lack of privacy, we all got along.

One evening I came back to our room after lights-out. Mindful of my sleeping roommates, I was standing at the sink, taking great care to wash up without a sound. Suddenly, a woman I'd not seen before leaped out of her bunk and violently accosted me. She was screaming wildly and gesturing toward my face, raging that I had disturbed her rest. Then she yanked open one of the vanity drawers and grabbed a vial of pills. Still yelling, she poured out a handful, flung them into her mouth, and, glaring at me, turned around and stomped back to her bed.

I was so stunned, I stood there in shock. These were the days before mobile phones, and it was the middle of the night, so even if it had occurred to me to call the security department, I had no way to do that. My other roommates, who might have offered support, had managed to sleep through the entire incident. So I was basically alone. Not knowing what else to do, I climbed into my bed and lay there the rest of the night, afraid she might attack me if I fell asleep.

I got up a few hours later, dressed quickly, and left the room. Days in the ashram always started the same way: morning meditation, followed by chai, followed by morning chanting, followed by breakfast. So I had several hours to process what had happened. By the time I finished my cereal, I knew I had to request a room change. To you, this may seem a no-brainer. I'd been violently accosted by a stranger who'd claimed the bunk above mine. I had every right to protect myself. But I was still hardwired to put other people's needs ahead of my own. Up until my post-cereal moment of clarity, the wounding masculine voice inside my head was weaponizing this stranger's action against me with messaging like: *You shouldn't say anything. You don't want to go behind her back. You'll get her in trouble. What about your other roommates, it's not right to abandon them. You need to deal with this yourself.*

Although my Kālī awareness was in its infancy, it was stirring. Terrifying as it was to stand up for my own safety, I went to the management office. Even then, the wounding masculine's messaging did not let up. *They'll think you're weak. They won't respect you. They won't believe you. You'll get in trouble.*

Instead of that censorious scenario however, here's what happened. The manager listened to my story and made a phone call. The next thing I knew, two lovely women appeared, walked me to my room, helped me pack my things, and moved me down the hall. Remember how I said the original room was small and dark? The new room was large, bright, and, miracle of miracles, had no roommates. A day or two after this welcome change, I came back to my new room and there was a note on the bed. It was from the woman who'd accosted me, apologizing for what she'd done. It turned out they'd told her that if she wished to remain in the ashram, she'd need to meet daily with a staff counselor.

Later that day I saw the one roommate who, it turned out, had witnessed the entire event but was too terrified to speak. Rather than being mad at me for "abandoning" her, she apologized for not supporting me. And then, the following week, I was taking a walk and the woman who'd threatened me was also on the path. We didn't say anything to each other. There really were no words. She nodded and smiled at me, I smiled back, and we both kept walking.

om srī kālī mā

Kālī is the power of our deep belly wisdom. It always has our back. It never lies. It simply wants us living from our deepest truth. It is fearless and often doesn't remember that we are not. Because of this it has a way of pushing us out of the comfortable ruts we'd rather stay stuck in. We may kick and scream the entire way, but sooner or later, we'll go. In the end, Kālī always wins.

Kālī on the Warpath

Adele was diagnosed with breast cancer and had to take medical leave from her job as a director at a pharmaceutical company. When she returned to the office, they'd done a reorganization and she was now reporting to a clueless bully with impossible expectations and terrible management skills. This would be challenging for anyone. For Adele, it was traumatic. Whereas before her cancer diagnosis she'd thought of herself as a strong, capable woman, now she was filled with anxiety and self-doubt. This erosion of her self-esteem, combined with exhaustion from surgery and chemo, terror of losing her job and health insurance, and the difficulties of managing an insane workload and insensitive boss, were keeping her in a constant state of panic and overwhelm. Because she was already on so many medications, she was hesitant to add an anti-anxiety to the mix, so her oncologist suggested she come see me for inner work.

Adele came for her first session soon after her return to the office. We talked about the nightmare of her cancer diagnosis and treatment, the egregious situation at work, and the sense of powerlessness that was consuming her. I told her that I certainly understood why she was feeling so wretched, adding that in these circumstances anyone would. I went on to say that I had a pretty strong sense that at her core, she was a warrior and would triumph. I could feel the fire smoldering inside her. It just needed to be reignited.

Adele was already practicing mindfulness meditation as part of her treatment plan. I suggested she add the mantra *om srī kālī mā* to her practice, silently repeating it on the in-breath and the out. She tried this and liked the way it felt, so she kept at it for several minutes.

I told her she might think of Kālī as the energy of a fierce mother bear protecting her young, and that working with this mantra would foster that same energy inside of her. She liked this idea and agreed to do the practice for five or ten minutes a few times each day. Adele left our first session feeling more hopeful, and we continued meeting weekly for the next few months.

Nothing much was changing in the workplace. If anything, her boss's behavior was more egregious than before. She was, however, beginning to see him clearly and learning to dodge his poison bullets. In the meantime, we continued working, talking, doing Eyes-Closed Work, and deepening her practice with the Kālī mantra. It was a joy to watch her reclaim herself, to see that smoldering inner fire begin to blaze. She was doing so well we decided to take a break and had no contact for several weeks. When she returned, she told me this story.

Her team had been up against an impossible deadline, made worse by the incessant demands of her bullying boss. While they'd managed to deliver on time, rather than taking responsibility for his poor management, her boss threw her under the bus. So when the call came from HR and the meeting did not go well, she was sure she was about to be fired.

She spent the next few hours in a paralysis of panic and self-doubt. And then, an upsurge of fury shot through her, and the next thing she knew, she was writing a letter—a very strong, clearly articulated letter, refuting his allegations. A week or two later she was once again summoned to HR. As it turned out, they were so impressed by her letter that they decided to move her to another department where she'd be working with a new boss, who, no big surprise, turned out to be a much better fit.

As she got to the end of this story, we were both laughing. While I knew she understood what had happened, I thought it best to state the obvious: "Needless to say, that upsurge of fury was your Kālī on fire!"

"Oh yes," she said. "I got that!"

om srī kālī mā

Experiences like these often have a sense of magic about them. One moment we're on the chopping block. The next, we're given a new lease on life. This is not magic. This is the clarifying power of the energy field personified as the goddess Kālī.

In Adele's situation, her Kālīesque fury broke open the insight she needed to remember herself. The next thing she knew, she was firing off the letter that not only saved her job, it actually made everything better. Putting pen to paper cut through the patriarch's paralyzing hold on her mind. Once that happened, her true masculine rose up, becoming the vehicle through which the clarity of her rage was perfectly articulated. This was a moment of "right identification" with her true masculine (rather than "wrong identification" with the voice of the inner patriarch), which fostered perfect integration with her feminine ground (in this case, the protective power of Kālī).

And that, my friends, is the winning formula for navigating the ups and downs of daily life, and if we can reach a tipping point, of saving this planet we all call home.

> When Kālī takes its rightful place inside us, the masculine finds its proper shape inside us and becomes what it is meant to be: a vehicle for truth, justice, compassion, and love in the world.

Unmasking the Imagery of Kālī

On the surface, the iconography of Kālī is terrifying. Often pictured holding a sword in one hand and severed head in another, she wears a garland of human skulls and belt of human arms. Her tongue lolls from her mouth and, apart from her gruesome adornments, she is quite naked, primal blackness, dancing on the corpse-like form of her other half, Lord Śiva.

This outer appearance is a veil. Her sword is the sword of discrimination, cutting away layers of wrong identification and clinging ego, all the sticky stuff that clouds our way. The severed head represents the patriarchal masculine and all the small-self characters it creates: caustic inner tyrant, complaining victim, life-squelching addict, narcissistic frenemy, damning judge. Kālī's sword dismembers these aberrations, making space for the true masculine to claim its rightful place in body, heart, and mind.

Kālī's garland of skulls symbolizes the power to speak the truth, and her belt of arms, the power to serve that truth. Her lolling tongue grounds her as she dances, and the corpse is not a corpse at all. In their sacred union of masculine and feminine, Śiva represents the container of inner stillness, while Kālī is the power of truth that rises from that stillness.

Kālī is also Time, the Great Matrix from which we are born and live our lives, and die back into again. Any wisdom path or psychology built around the goddess begins here. The goddess is a metaphor for unity and wholeness, for relationship and connection. The goddess is about power and possibility. Not power over others. Never power over others. The goddess is the power of being and of belonging to each other, in wisdom, compassion, and love.

Kālī is also Time, the Great Matrix from which we are born and live our lives, and die back into again. Any wisdom path or psychology built around the goddess begins here. The goddess is a metaphor for unity and wholeness, for relationship and connection. The goddess is about power and possibility. Not power over others. Never power over others. The goddess is the power of being and of belonging to each other, in wisdom, compassion, and love.

I'm sure that anyone reading this book is well aware that our planet is in crisis, thanks to human greed, avoidance, and denial. We are the cause of every problem we face, from environmental catastrophe; to racial, gender, and economic injustice; to planetary pandemics; to poverty, hunger, lack of clean water, overcrowding, forced migration, war, militarized police, plastic pollution, fossil fuel rape of the earth, holocaust against Indigenous peoples, global misery, suffering, and despair—to name just a handful off the top of my head.

None of us can single-handedly right these wrongs. This is a collective endeavor requiring an international army of Kālīesque warriors pushing back against the madness that is normalized in the patriarchal paradigm. What we can do, however, at the individual level, is address the patriarchal masculine inside of ourselves.

We can learn to recognize it in all its wily ways and meet this destructive inner force with the fierce awareness of our Kālī self. This is how we transform the patriarch into a strong and healthy masculine, a vibrant and vital masculine, a masculine that stands for and stands in love. And a loving masculine in partnership with the deep feminine is the human possibility that can restore, redeem, and reenchant our world.

> This is how we transform the patriarch into a strong and healthy masculine, a vibrant and vital masculine, a masculine that stands for and stands in love. And a loving masculine in partnership with the deep feminine is the human possibility that can restore, redeem, and reenchant our world.

The Terrible and The Beautiful

In 1977, when I was twenty-nine years old, I attended my first meditation retreat with the guru whose path I would walk for much of the next two decades. Among the many questions on my mind, what plagued me most was confusion about my music. Sometimes it was so tender and lyrical, I couldn't believe such beauty was coming through me. Other times, it was pounding and wild, screaming with a raging power that scared me. Yet when I was in it, I felt utterly serene. This made no sense, and afterward, the shame and doubt, the need to keep it secret, would come.

Now I was at this retreat, hoping to find answers to who I was and what this raging music was all about. During one of the meditation sessions, I stumbled into the liminal space beyond the mind. This is a place where sacred conversations happen, where past, present, and future meld into one. It is also, in her attribute as Time, Kālī's domain.

I don't remember how the conversation started. And by conversation, I'm not talking about chatting with another human being. This was an encounter with an inner presence that had no visual form but exuded a palpable power. While I no longer remember all that passed between us, I've never forgotten the awe I felt. I spoke of many things, most importantly, of how I feared there was a dangerous force inside me. How else to explain the strange dichotomy in my music, how it could shift from tender beauty to raging screams. And then the voice spoke. Not so much in words, it spoke in the language of that place—a language way deeper than words, way deeper than the mind. It is a language of insight, a language of awe, a language that leaves an indelible mark on the heart.

This was forty-five years ago. I still feel the touch of that place, its shimmering darkness, the stillness there, my sense of being in the presence of overwhelming power and great kindness: *Your music is the song of earth and sky, of thunder and lightning, of earthquakes and volcanoes. It is the dark depths of the ocean and blazing light of the sun. It is birds soaring, the majesty of trees, the aroma of roses and jasmine, the loving heart. You sing the terrible and the beautiful. It is all one. Do not fear or doubt it. It is all one. It is all one.*

As far as liminal-space conversations go, this one was up there on the "aha" scale. For years I assumed the presence with whom I "spoke" had been my guru. Much later I realized that while he may have opened a portal, this was the voice of my innate Kālī.

om srī kālī mā

The Great Matrix That Is Ultimately Made of Love

I was talking with a friend the other day, telling her that I was writing this story, sharing it publicly for the first time. We laughed at how, for me, it always resolves in Kālī. No matter how I long to luxuriate with Lakṣmī, sing with Saraswatī, or bathe in Kuan Yin's waters, it is always Kālī who is my default operating system, the motherboard, the internal alignment I recognize as home.

And perhaps this is the best way to work with these archetypes. Find the one you recognize as home. Lean into it, learn from it, listen to it, love it. It will gentle you through the agonies and the ecstasies, the sublime and the mundane, the terrible and the beautiful.

It will also open gates to the other three. While one may seem to be the strongest inside you, they are all intimately connected. They flow in and out of one another, balancing, fortifying, energizing, enlivening, and most of all, perhaps, enjoying each other's company. Which is really the company of our very own self.

We're conditioned to seek outside ourselves for meaning, for value, for love, tricked into believing that the grass over there is greener, and that if we can just have that other grass, our lives will be so much better. Then we get that grass, and it turns out nothing has changed, except now we have more to take care of and more to lose. Which is not to say there is anything wrong with growing grass—just that we need to remember to also grow the grass inside ourselves.

This grass will grow and stretch and spread our beauty everywhere. So that when death—who is also known as the terrible, who is also known as time, who is also known as reality—comes for that grass, it will leave a blessing in its place. When we do harm to ourselves or to any other cell within the Great Matrix, we risk offending the blessing. And only the patriarch is so foolhardy as to take that risk.

Chapter 10

LAKṢMĪ

The multiplicity of forms! The hummingbird,
the fox, the raven, the sparrow hawk, the otter,
the dragonfly, the water lily! And on and on.
It must be a great disappointment to God
if we are not dazzled at least ten times a day.
—Mary Oliver

We live in a system that wants us believing financial wealth is the key to happiness. This is a ridiculous notion, but it does keep the wheels of global capitalism spinning. However, I digress. We're here to talk about Lakṣmī, an aspect of the goddess often associated with this wrongheaded notion that financial wealth = happiness. I therefore begin her chapter with a small diatribe to make the point that equating wealth with happiness and bundling Lakṣmī into the equation is yet another lie of the patriarchal project. Nothing could be further from the truth.

Here's what Lakṣmī is: an energy field of infinite possibility infused with love. Love. Not greed, ambition, or desire. Love. The way she's commonly drawn, with gold coins flowing from her hands, really does create the wrong impression. This is not to say there's anything wrong with having a stash of gold coins (sustainably mined and minted of course). The problem is equating those coins with long-term happiness. The truth is, we can lose them in an instant. Which is why all the world's wisdom traditions agree that it's better to find happiness at its source: inside ourselves.

> Real poverty is the belief that the purpose of life is acquiring wealth and owning things. Real wealth is not the possession of property but the recognition that our deepest need as human beings is to keep developing our natural and acquired powers to relate to other human beings.
> —*Grace Lee Boggs*

> Poverty is not a character failing or a lack of motivation. Poverty is a shortage of money.
> —*Barbara Ehrenreich*

Lakṣmī and the Hummingbirds

Lakṣmī is the joy we feel on a beautiful day. We can also say that Lakṣmī *is* the beautiful day. This is an energy field that animates everything it touches with that shimmering sense of grace we experience in those "life doesn't get any better" moments. Whatever Lakṣmī touches does get better, becoming finer, truer, deeper, more beautiful. Some of the words associated with this archetypal field are auspiciousness, beauty, magnificence, grace, expansion, fertility, vitality, and serenity.

I had a sublime Lakṣmī moment the other day. It was early evening, and I was sitting outside. After a long summer with no respite from the heat, finally it was cool. Soft breeze. Leaves gently stirring. Setting sun casting everything in golden light. It was one of those "life doesn't get any better" moments.

And then it did.

Two hummingbirds landed on the feeder that hangs on a tree near my deck, a blue jay landed on a nearby limb, and the four of us sat there in holy communion: the hummingbirds sipping their nectar, the blue jay nibbling on a chunk of bread, and me sipping a glass of iced rosé. I felt such wonder and delight, such awe in the presence in and around us, and then thought, *Ah, this is Lakṣmī.*

Over the many years I've taught about the goddess, whenever I offer Lakṣmī workshops, they always sell out. This is because of the association with material abundance. Far too many people believe that if they just chant enough Lakṣmī mantras, financial wealth will accrue. Would that it were so easy. In order for Lakṣmī to take a seat at our table, we need to seriously clean house, inner and outer, and then invite everyone to the feast.

The Birth of Lakṣmī: The Great Churning

Lakṣmī's creation myth offers a step-by-step guide for how to do this. The myth has multiple sources. The one most often cited is found in *Srimad Bhagavatam.* Although there are numerous tellings and retellings, the basic gist remains the same. Here's a pared-down version:

The war between the gods and demons had been going on for many years when the gods, greatly weakened by the fighting, sought Lord Viṣnu's counsel. Listening to their plight, he told them that in order to win this war, they needed the ambrosial dew of life—it's called amrita*—which could only be obtained by churning the Ocean of Milk. There was a catch, though. They couldn't churn alone. They had to churn together with the demons. "When there is a great task ahead," Viṣnu added, "one should befriend even enemies. One's object is more easily achieved by kindness than by anger."*

And so, as an audience of thousands looked on, the gods and demons took their places and the great churning began. At first, a wondrous array of divine and celestial beings arose, filling everyone with delight. But then, a cloud of poison pushed through. Fortunately Lord Śiva *was watching the spectacle. Realizing that if he didn't act quickly the toxic vapors would kill all they touched, he reached into the foaming milk, scooped up the poison, and drank it. This sacrificial act saved the assembled multitudes but nearly killed him.*

Seeing her supreme lord's throat turning blue, Pārvatī (who is a gentler form of Kālī) took him onto her lap and rocked him back to life. Only then did the miracle happen. Lakṣmī arose, seated on a lotus flower, its long stem rooted in the mud of the ocean floor. Holding an urn filled with the precious dew of life, she walked out of the milky sea, beautiful and serene, and as she took her place beside Viṣnu, a great stillness was everywhere.

om śrī lakṣmī mā

We can say that Lakṣmī lives in abundance but not all abundance is Lakṣmī, that Lakṣmī lives in beauty but not all beauty is Lakṣmī, that Lakṣmī lives in gracefulness but not all gracefulness is Lakṣmī. The myth is very clear about this. In order to realize our Lakṣmī possibility, we have to be willing to wrestle with (aka churn) all the stuff inside us: what we like and what we don't, what we see and what we look away from, what we know and what lurks deep in the unconscious. We have to drink the poisons of hatred, unworthiness, shame, and greed, always knowing that if we drink too much, we can sit in the lap of being and be restored. Only then can we meet ourselves (and the world) in all our richness and power.

Not All Abundance Is Lakṣmī

I grew up in the financial abundance of the postwar era. All that abundance notwithstanding, our family home did not overflow with Lakṣmī. My parents' approach to life was to get everything over and done with as quickly as possible. Speed and efficiency were their mantras, because time was money. I was never taught to enjoy the simple pleasure of working thoroughly, carefully, and dare I say it, lovingly. Quality and beauty were not in the lesson plan.

Before landing on the yogic path, I spent some time on an inner path known as the Gurdjieff Work. Mindfulness—which was referred to as "self-remembering"—was an essential part of the program. We met on a farm, so working in the gardens was one of the places we did our self-remembering practice. Early in my sojourn, I was assigned to pull weeds from a flower bed. I think this was the first time in my life I was given a task that was not about finishing. It was simply about the quality of my attention as I pulled those weeds.

When I was growing up I never much liked weeding or, for that matter, any of the chores I had to do. Cleaning my room, doing my homework, practicing the piano, these were all tedious tasks to get through as quickly as possible. I had no idea I could relax into and actually enjoy what I was doing, never mind do it really well. Instead, I always felt a subtle anxiety pushing me to finish. It was a pressure that always hung over me. Like I was in a rush to get somewhere that, truth be told, was generally nowhere.

This brought a brutality to my relationship with time that became my default mode. So when I was assigned this weeding job in the garden, I felt a surge of anxiety. Sitting there, however, letting my mind become absorbed in what I was doing, in doing purely for doing's sake, I found myself actually enjoying the work.

The more carefully I pulled a weed, the more tenderly I placed it in the weed bucket, the more relaxed I felt. It was as if each weed, lovingly pulled, opened up more space inside me. And there was no anxiety in that spaciousness. There was, much to my astonishment, joy. It was so simple. In order to enjoy what I'd previously eschewed, all I had to do was relax, get out of my head, get into my body, and rather than rushing to finish, just focus on whatever it was I was doing.

For me, this was revelatory, a whole new model for how to live. Viewed through the analytical frame of this book, we can say that before this experience, my doing function was ruled by a patriarchal masculine that squeezed all possibility of joyous engagement from my relationship with any kind of work. Instead it kept me goal oriented and wrongly identified with pressure and anxiety. Being given "permission" to do for the sake of doing, with no agenda beyond paying careful attention, opened me into an anxiety-free state. Once the anxiety was removed, my healthy doing function kicked in, opening me into a profound sense of spaciousness and joy, into a sense of right identification or perfect integration of doing and being.

The Beautiful Mud

For the record, time is not money and money is not time. Kālī is Time. And Lakṣmī is the spaciousness inside of time. Lakṣmī lives in the art of paying attention, of stretching into the details and pleasure of slowing down. I'm reminded of Aesop's fable "The Tortoise and the Hare." Yes, the tortoise wins. Yes, the moral of the story is slow and steady wins the race. And yet, if you're honest with yourself, who would you rather be? The plodding, funny-looking tortoise or the lean, graceful hare?

Moral be damned, most of us secretly admire the hare. It's our patriarchal conditioning. We'd rather be lean and mean than round and close to the ground. But round and close to the ground is a lot closer to Lakṣmī. Another name for the goddess is the Great Round. And let us remember what is holding the lotus that Lakṣmī sits on. Lakṣmī, not to mention all creation, is rooted in the mud.

> And let us remember what is holding the lotus that Lakṣmī sits on. Lakṣmī, not to mention all creation, is rooted in the mud.

My first trip to the ashram in India coincided with Diwali, the five-day Hindu festival of light. Diwali is associated with Lakṣmī, and on the third day, a ceremony—it's called Lakṣmī Puja—begins at dusk. This is a beautiful ritual. In the ashram it goes on for hours. Hundreds of candles and small lamps are lit, mantras are chanted, and many offerings—rice, spices, fruits, sweets, gemstones, silks, gold jewelry—are made to the goddess. It's traditional to wear one's best clothes for Lakṣmī Puja. I was wearing a brand-new silk sari.

The puja was held in a large grassy field. By the time it ended, night had fallen. I hadn't thought to bring a flashlight, so I walked back to the women's dorm in the dark. It was a perfect evening.

The air was cool. The sky was filled with stars. The moon was full. Monsoon had recently ended and the moist ground felt wonderful on my bare feet. I felt so happy and serene, so grateful to be in this place at this time, light as a feather and filled with a rapturous sense of well-being.

And then I stumbled and slipped on a pile of muddy cow dung. Barefoot and draped in my new silk sari on a pile of muddy cow dung. Mushy, muddy cow dung oozing over my feet and splashing onto my beautiful new silk sari.

It was a moment . . .

Then I remembered a talk I'd heard earlier that day, where I learned that Lakṣmī lives in cow dung. In India one goes to the guru, shrine, or temple to receive a blessing. It's called *darshan*, which literally translates as "to have the sight of." That night, splattered with muddy dung, I received the full darshan of Lakṣmī, and returned to my room, blessed from head to toe and laughing all the way.

om śrī lakṣmī mā

Every part of our personality that we do not love will become hostile to us.
—Robert Bly

The Self
pushes the neglected forward
for recognition.
Do not disregard it.
It holds energy
of highest value.
It is the gold in the dung.
Do not disregard the dung.
—Marion Woodman

With beauty before me may I walk.
With beauty behind me may I walk.
With beauty below me may I walk.
With beauty above me may I walk.
With beauty all around me may I walk.
—*Navajo Blessing Way Ceremony*

Mulla Nasrudin decided to start a flower garden. He prepared the soil and planted the seeds of many beautiful flowers. But when they came up, his garden was filled not just with his chosen flowers but was also overrun by dandelions. He sought advice from gardeners all over and tried every method known to get rid of them, but to no avail. Finally he walked all the way to the capital to speak to the royal gardener at the sheik's palace. The wise old man had counseled many gardeners before and suggested a variety of remedies to expel the dandelions but Mulla had tried them all.

They sat together in silence for some time and finally the gardener looked at Nasrudin and said, "Well, then I suggest you learn to love them."
—*Sufi tale*

Where Lakṣmī Lives

Lakṣmī lives in the spaciousness of kindness and generosity, in the welcoming embrace of life. Lakṣmī lives in beauty, inner and outer, and in the calling from deep within of the very best we are. We could say that Lakṣmī *is* the best we are. Inside, outside, and all around us.

Ultimately, Lakṣmī lives in the love that binds us together, the love that is so much wiser than our binary categories of black and white, right and wrong, nectar and dung, my way or the highway. To live in the energy field of Lakṣmī, to have right identification with this energy field is, as the Navajo prayer reminds us, to walk in beauty, to move through life with a sense that even on the hardest days, even during the most difficult times, we know that we are held.

As I write these words, my inner patriarch whispers this critique: "Easy for you to say. Your life has been so privileged. What about someone working hours in brutal, inhumane conditions? What about someone held in prison, trapped in a refugee camp, caught in a war zone or in human trafficking? What about someone who is severely ill, has endured terrible trauma, or is living in impossible conditions with no clear way out? How can you say that anyone in these situations is 'held'? How can you say, when you look around and see the destruction that humans inflict on one another and the planet, that there is such a thing as being held?"

It's a good point. And one that should be made. I'm reminded, however, of Albert Woodfox, a man you may never have heard of, who in my opinion embodies exactly what I'm talking about.

Albert Woodfox and Lakṣmī

In 1965 Woodfox, a member of the Black Panther Party, was tried and found guilty of a murder he did not commit. Even though that faulty conviction was overturned multiple times, he remained incarcerated for five decades, spending nearly forty-four of those years in solitary confinement. Woodfox was finally released from prison in 2016. Here's a quote from an interview he gave three years later.

> You know, throughout all this, I developed an unbelievable love for humanity and dedicated myself to doing whatever I can to better humanity. I remember reading something

> from Mr. Mandela, and he said, "If a cause is noble, you can carry the weight of the world on your shoulders." And I thought what we were doing was a noble cause. So we were prepared. And so the beatings and the gassings and the decades of solitary confinement, you know, was really—although painful and difficult, it never got to the point where they were able to break us. . .

For a man to walk out of prison, having spent fifty-plus years there, forty-four of them in solitary confinement, and say that through it all he developed an unbelievable love for humanity, is, in my opinion, an extraordinary expression of the nobility of soul that so embodies Lakṣmī. We may not live into or up to it, we may besmirch and turn away from it, we may die having never experienced a glimpse of its radiance. But nobility of soul is part of our birthright. Even in the most challenging circumstances, we can rest there. And beauty, nobility, and love are primary colors of the archetypal power that is Lakṣmī.

> The God, who is greater than God, has only one thing on Her mind, and that is to drop, endlessly, rose petals on our heads.
>
> —*Gregory Boyle*

Lakṣmī, Alakṣmī, and Dhūmāvatī

Lakṣmī has two nonidentical twin sisters. Their names are Alakṣmī and Dhūmāvatī. In order to fully embody our Lakṣmī possibility, we have to embrace these two. We'll come back to Dhūmāvatī in Part III. For now, let's focus on Alakṣmī.

In Sanskrit, when an "a" is placed before a noun, it denotes the absence or negation of that which the noun is naming. So Alakṣmī comes to be understood as where Lakṣmī is not. If you do an online search of Alakṣmī, you'll see that she is often drawn as an emaciated old crone with sunken cheeks and beady eyes. You'll find descriptions that say she is a goddess of misfortune, poverty, laziness, and greed; that she resides wherever there is dirt, filth, crime, poverty, illness, and suffering. Any number of sources will add that she brings jealousy and malice into a household and that ruin follows in her wake.

Now let me just say on Alakṣmī's behalf—not that she needs my support—that most of these attributes have nothing to do with the goddess. So for starters, let's set the record straight and remind ourselves that it's the human mind formed in patriarchy that's responsible for the dirt, filth, crime, poverty, illness, suffering, and greed that is such a blight on planet Earth. Let's not let the true villains get away with blaming our societal ills on Alakṣmī. She has nothing to do with them.

The goddess is a paradigm of wholeness. Wholeness. As in nonduality. As in One. As in the One Great Round of Everything. As in it's all connected, as in we're all connected. There is, in reality, no division. The patriarchal diseases of duality, hierarchy, bipolarity, cruelty, and ranking are an aberration brought to us by human persons determined to deny reality.

> The goddess is a paradigm of wholeness. Wholeness. As in nonduality. As in One. As in the One Great Round of Everything. As in it's all connected, as in we're all connected. There is, in reality, no division. The patriarchal diseases of duality, hierarchy, bipolarity, cruelty, and ranking are an aberration brought to us by human persons determined to deny reality.

Most every deity in Hindu mythology is associated with an animal that is called their vehicle or mount. For example, if you look at the iconography, you'll often see Viṣnu with Garuda the eagle, Śiva with Nandi the bull, or Gaṇeśa with Mushika the mouse. Lakṣmī's mount is the white owl. If you dig a little deeper into Alakṣmī, you'll begin to find references where she's drawn as an owl. And not just any owl. You'll see Alakṣmī drawn as the white owl that is Lakṣmī's mount.

Let's take a moment to contemplate this curious symbolism. If Lakṣmī is the power of infinite possibility infused with love, of sublime magnificence, beauty, majesty, and grace, and Alakṣmī is the absence of all these, why would she be found anywhere near Lakṣmī? For that matter, why would Lakṣmī choose her to be her mount? And why would this cadaverous hag be portrayed as a magnificent white owl?

The commentators get around this by saying that the mount represents that which the deity destroys. Nice try, but too simplistic. Especially in the case of Lakṣmī, who is not in the business of destroying anything. Let's remember that in her primary cosmic role, Lakṣmī is the sustainer, not the destroyer. No, all these attributes assigned to Alakṣmī—dirt, filth, crime, poverty, etc.—are consequences of the patriarchal project. To blame them on Alakṣmī is a misogynistic denial of the perpetrator's responsibility. Something that is much more profound is going on beneath the surface of the patriarchal lens through which these myths are told.

Alakṣmī is the wide-open spaciousness of Lakṣmī, a spaciousness we want to keep pristine, so there is no place for the wounding masculine to sink its claws. At her core, Alakṣmī is the stillness of stillness, the Great Void. This is where the notion of Alakṣmī as the vehicle of Lakṣmī makes sense. What better vehicle to carry the infinite possibility that is infused with love than the wide-open stillness of stillness? Anything else may have an agenda, and where an agenda lurks, the inner patriarch will be hiding. And speaking of our old nemesis the wounding/wounded masculine, only that distortion of mind would turn the sublime mystery that is Alakṣmī into a craven and deformed old woman.

om śrī lakṣmī mā, om śrī alakṣmī mā

Owl Poem

One has to say this for the rounds of life
 that keep coming and going; it has worked so far.
The rabbit, after all, has never asked if the grass
 wanted to live.
Any more than the owl consults with the rabbit.

Acceptance of the world requires
 that I bow even to you,
Master of the night.
—*Mary Oliver*

Setting Lakṣmī's Table

I've worked with many couples in my private practice and was married myself for thirty years. Over and over, in my own life and in the lives of clients, loved ones, and friends, I've seen that most of the time, when we're having relationship problems, the root has to do with a contraction and stifling—I would go so far as to call it an oppression—of Lakṣmī's presence in the house.

One of the ways this showed itself in my long marriage was my husband's need to be right. This was a terrible burden for both of us. He was hard of hearing but refused to wear his hearing aids in the house. Because of this, when I came in he often didn't hear me say hello. This became one of his pet peeves. The fact that I had said hello didn't matter. His need to be right overrode the fact that his hearing loss was the reason he hadn't heard me.

Had he been willing to do the Lakṣmī work, rather than using his hearing loss as a weapon against me, we could have embraced it together. We could have come up with simple strategies to make it better for both of us. Alas, he was unable to go there. So his internal space was very cramped. No room for Lakṣmī. Too much room for the wounding masculine. And something as simple as not hearing me come into the house became cause for two days of resentment.

This kind of contracted inner space is fertile nurturing ground for the projections, assumptions, expectations, and narratives that are the wounding/wounded masculine's stock-in-trade. Every trigger and reaction to that trigger comes from the projection of something inside ourselves we have not recognized, befriended, and integrated, aka churned, into our sense of self.

This is important, so let me say it one more time: *Every trigger and reaction to that trigger comes from the projection of something inside ourselves we have not recognized, befriended, and integrated, aka churned, into our sense of self.*

Feeling jealousy, judgment, or dislike for another? Take a good hard look at yourself and see what they're mirroring in you. This is how we welcome Lakṣmī, set the table, and invite everyone to the feast.

> You stand with the least likely to succeed until success is succeeded by something more valuable: kinship. You stand with . . . the badly behaved until bad behavior is recognized for the language it is: the vocabulary of the deeply wounded and of those whose burdens are more than they can bear.
> —*Gregory Boyle*

Our Projections Are Such a Bore

In the 1990s and early aughts, I was traveling with a small band of musicians, offering chanting concerts and workshops up and down the East Coast. One Saturday, we arrived for a gig at a yoga center. The teacher who'd presented the week before, a person with a large international following, was still in the house. I was in the changing room when I overheard him talking on his cell phone, ranting about money and belittling his followers. Gone was his pious public persona. In its place, just another greedy grifter.

Initially I was shocked. My shock quickly turned into revulsion, which channeled into judgment, which morphed into nonstop narratives of what a phony he was. This went on for a while until I realized that maybe, rather than focusing on him, I should look at my own harsh judgments. These were not a pretty sight. I had to admit that underneath the judgment, I was jealous of his fame, and underneath the jealousy, and even more disturbing to acknowledge, I saw that he was a mirror of my greatest fear: that I was an impostor. As uncomfortable as it was to face this, once I owned up, all the judgments ceased. I realized it was all projection. Greedy grifter he might be, but that had nothing to do with me. It was way more interesting to look at my own jealousy and self-doubt and to clean up that mess.

Living under the influence of our projections is such a bore. So much better to follow Śiva's playbook and drink the poison. Although when it comes to projections, I always have the idea we should eat, not drink them. Eat, drink, whichever you prefer. Everyone is invited to this feast. What matters is hosting the meal.

I know it can seem terrifying to look at all the inner stuff we think we'd rather not see. Turns out, it's way more dangerous not to look. Leaning into what actually is, even when we dread going down that rabbit hole, turns out to be the way we open up more space inside. It's in this ever-widening spaciousness that we discover, recover, and ultimately rest in the shimmering luminosity and fertile darkness, in the impeccable splendor, of our inner ground.

Why would we ever want to cut ourselves off from that?

> She is Light itself . . . Emanating from Her body are rays in thousands—two thousand, a hundred thousand, tens of millions, a hundred million—there is no counting their numbers. It is by and through Her that all things moving and motionless shine . . .
> —*Bhairava Yamala*

Being Alive Is Messy, Complicated, and Filled with Contradiction

When I was still young in my journey, I bought into a binary dogma filled with judgment and rules. I was so hung up on notions of what is pure and what is not, of what is good and what is bad, that I missed the experience of being alive. Being alive is messy and complicated and filled with contradiction. And that is okay. Being alive is about diving and soaring and everything in between, about opening into the Mystery that does not give a damn about the categories in which we try to organize it. Separating ourselves from the vastness of our humanity, pointing our finger at the other, is the surest way to banish Lakṣmī from our lives.

I remember visiting a friend who'd recently moved to a new town. In those days I was eating a strict vegan diet with no refined foods, no sugar or dairy, no animal products or plastic in the house. No shoes, radio, or TV either. Definitely no microwave. I wouldn't even read *The New York Times*, go to the movies, or open a book that was not Eastern philosophy or sacred poetry.

My friend brought me to a bakery some friends of hers had just opened. It was a temple of white flour, white sugar, eggs, whipped cream, and butter. It was charming, beautiful, and the smells were divine. All I experienced, however, was revulsion, mortified to be in the presence of such impurity. I even made an anti-white-sugar, anti-white-flour comment to the owners—oh yes, I was insufferable—all the time thinking I was this wonderfully pure person dispensing my great wisdom.

My friend and I walked out of the bakery together. She was furious. How could I have been so rude? I'd insulted her friends and embarrassed her. She wanted nothing to do with me and walked off in a huff. I continued to my car, shocked by her awful behavior. I was building a strong case against her when a wave of insight ripped through me. I realized that if anyone's behavior in this mix was awful, it was mine. It wasn't about what I ate or what

I chose to avoid. It was about loving and embracing the world. And that included white flour and white sugar. And people who ate white flour and white sugar. And people who got mad at me for being such a pompous fool. How could I be pure when my mind was filled with judgment? If anything, purity grew in a mind that was free of rigidity and dogma. Purity was forged in love. Love of self, love of other.

om śrī lakṣmī mā

Living with Eyes Wide Open

I wish I could tell you I was able to hold the insight I had that day. That took many more years. An immune disorder that corrected itself when my physician ordered me to eat beef, chicken, eggs, and fish certainly helped. As did watching the woman who taught me macrobiotics develop anorexia. And seeing my vegan Tai Chi teacher secretly devour a plate of scrambled eggs. Apologizing to my friend for being such a holier-than-thou ninny was also a step in the right direction. As was raising a teenager who just wanted to be normal, and showed me, over and over, the limitations of my spiritual grandiosity. Ultimately, it was through the process of inner churning that I came to understand that for me, the spiritual path lay in embracing the world as it is, not as I believe it should be.

> God would seem to be too occupied in being unable to take Her eyes off of us to spend any time raising an eyebrow in disapproval.
> —*Gregory Boyle*

Lakṣmī personifies the force that sustains all creation. This is a stance that requires undivided attention. Look away for a moment and the whole world may disappear. Which is why Lakṣmī never closes her eyes. The essence of Lakṣmī is about living with eyes wide open. It's about opening to the world, about cherishing all life, about embodying the nobility that rises from the mud. It is limitless possibility. It is unconditional love. It is the impeccable splendor.

> Your glance is wide, auspicious, the base for the flow of kindness, tender, with love toward all. The learned have said that by the opening and closing of your eyes, the universe is created and destroyed. Hence, in order to protect this entire universe, your eyes remain ever open.
> *—Traditional Devotional Song to Lakṣmī*

Five Simple Ways to Welcome Lakṣmī into Daily Life

1. Offer an act of kindness to yourself, to a loved one, to a neighbor or friend, to a stranger, to the person who delivers your mail, to the person at the register at the grocery store, or better yet, to the person in front of you who is taking forever to bag their stuff. Anyone will do. Might be as simple as giving them a great big smile. A smile rooted in the depths of your heart. A smile that really means it. A smile that says I see you and am enriched in that seeing.

2. Choose a spot in your living space. Clean it until it sparkles. Large or small. It doesn't matter. However it looks right now, make it shine.

3. Make and serve a wonderful meal for yourself or for a group of people you know.

4. Treat yourself to something special, something that makes you smile. Not because you're looking for happiness in externals. Only for the sheer joy of being alive. And while you're at it, grab something special for someone you know.

5. Share your wealth. Gift a friend or stranger who's in need. Support organizations working to make the world a better place. Live a life that makes the world a better place. Support local farmers and patronize independent businesses. Even if you have only a few gold coins, even if you have only one, share a penny. And if that is more than you have, take a long, deep breath, and on your exhale, send a wave of love to someone who has less than you.

Chapter 11

SARASWATĪ

Finally I saw that worrying had come to nothing.
And gave it up. And took my old body and
went into the morning, and sang.
—Mary Oliver

Here's what the texts will tell you about Saraswatī. In the earliest stirrings, she's visualized as a river goddess whose waters cleanse and fertilize the earth. Over time, her physical waters morph into an association with speech and sound, and from there with learning, eloquence, and the arts. Saraswatī personifies the power that flows through insight, inspiration, and intelligence. Described as the impeller of true and sweet speech and the awakener of happy and noble thoughts, my favorite epithet is Kavijihvāgrāvāsinī, "She who dwells on the tongues of poets."

Here's the fairy tale. There were once three sister goddesses. Their names were Gaṅgā, Lakṣmī, and Saraswatī. When they came of age, all three were given in marriage to Viṣnu. Lakṣmī was content in her new life. Saraswatī and Gaṅgā were not. So the three devised a plan. Gaṅgā and Saraswatī would feign a bitter feud between them. Lakṣmī would try to mediate and fail. And Viṣnu would send his warring wives away.

The plan worked. Lakṣmī remained with Viṣnu, while Gaṅgā and Saraswatī moved on, reclaiming their elemental river forms. Gaṅgā still flows today as Mother Ganges, the great holy river of India. As for Saraswatī, most say that some time around 3000 BCE her waters dried up and disappeared. The wise ones, however, tell it differently. They say the mighty Saraswatī transformed herself from a river of water to the river of inspiration, flowing through the human body, mind, heart, and soul.

And then there's the goddess herself. If asked to speak on her behalf, here's what I think she might say. *Read between the lines of these pretty stories. They veil me from your eyes. Look below the veils. See me as I am. I live in your mind, your belly, and your heart, in your blood and your bones. I am your voice. I have been repressed, suppressed, stolen from you and dismembered, hidden in iconography and mythic tales. I am not a sacred being you must worship from afar. I am the living power of insight, your insight, the living power of inspiration, your inspiration, the living power of intelligence, your intelligence. I belong to you.*

Visualize me any way you like. Young or old. Male or female. Everything in between. I live in your words, your silence, your actions. Do not allow the wounding forces inside you to stifle, crimp, or break me into so many pieces you barely feel my presence.

om srī saraswatī mā

The Voice

The voice calls us into the world. The voice calls us home to our self. It sings from the belly and the heart. It sings through the mind. It sings from every cell of every bone, in every drop, each molecule of blood and skin and hair. It sings in our smiles and our tears, in the silence between sound and the sound between silence.

Think about your voice. Say it out loud. MY VOICE. Then write down the words or phrases that come to you. Here are mine. Heart. Soul. Being. Tough. Hidden. Mysterious. Wonder. Who I am. What I say.

I find singing easier than writing. I sit down at the piano or harmonium, get a chordal drone going, open my mouth, and there it is. So fine and alive, so strong and sure of itself. Comfortable in the silence and the sound.

Writing is tougher for me. I have to reach into the knowing in my bones, bringing that knowing up and out, shaping it into words that will become coherent thoughts that will communicate to you what I feel so clearly inside myself. It's so much easier to sing.

This was not always the case. When I was growing up, I loved to sit at the piano and sing. Then people made fun of my voice. Which tricked me into believing there was something wrong with it. This was a terrible burden to place on a child. I lived with it quietly and with not a little bit of shame. I stopped singing solo when people were around. I sang only harmonies. I sang always quietly. I wanted no one to hear my voice. By the time I graduated from high school, it had mostly gone into hiding.

Finding My Voice

This began to shift after my daughter was born. I started singing when I nursed or rocked her to sleep. She seemed to like it. Which gave me courage. Slowly, I cracked open the door my voice was trapped behind. Slowly, I learned to let it wander and roam. Later on, when I became a professional singer, I was always stunned when people spoke of the beauty and power of my voice. It took me years to believe this might be true.

> *I am your voice. I am that which lives inside you and is expressed through your mouth, your actions, and the language of your body. I am the impulse that gives rise to all your expression. And I am that expression. I am everything you have ever thought of and not thought of, everything you have understood, understand, and will understand.*

In those early years when I was beginning to find my voice, a friend of a friend came to stay with us. She was older than we were, somewhere in her thirties, and had a stillness about her I'd never felt in anyone before. If I'd had the language at that time, I would have called her a Kālī woman. Mostly she scared me. I think she was a messenger. The problem was I was too frightened to receive the message.

I've thought of her over the years. I wish I could tell you her name. She had bright blue eyes, black hair, and was very beautiful. I always had the sense that she was watching me. I could tell she saw me more clearly than I saw myself. This terrified me. The shame still held me tight in its embrace.

This was the time when I'd started writing songs and working them out on the piano. I played softly so as not to disturb anyone. Even so, the house was often filled, ever so quietly, with my music. I came into the dining room one day when she was drinking tea. She invited me to join her. She was quiet for a few minutes, letting her stillness fill the room. Then she looked at me thoughtfully and said, "Do you understand you have a gift?" I looked at her quizzically. She went on, telling me how she'd been in rooms with two of the great female singer-songwriters of that time, and continued, "Do you understand you have what they have?" Then she looked at me with that look I found so discomfiting and asked, "Why are you hiding?"

Those words haunted me for years.

Shame Is a Terrible Filter

Shame is a terrible filter. It stifles our voice, stopping us in our tracks, distorting our sense of self, slowly crushing us. Shame is one of the most toxic weapons of the wounding masculine. It cloaks us in webs of doubt and self-loathing, muting our ability to live the truth of who we actually are. It pretends to protect us. It pretends it is our friend. It is not. It is the enemy. The silencer. The obliterator. In most of us, it lives right next to our voice, along with its sister, fear.

The physical throat and its energetic partner, the throat chakra, are the center of the voice. This is also the primary area of the body where shame and fear are stored. You know those dreams where you're being chased and try calling for help but you've lost your voice? I had those dreams for years.

When I was in my mid-thirties, my doctor noticed a swelling on the right side of my throat. This turned out to be an enlargement of my thyroid. About the size of a walnut, the thyroid is a butterfly-shaped gland that sits in front of the windpipe, close to the vocal cords and voice box. The butterfly wings are its right and left lobes. Although all the physicians I saw recommended surgery, I didn't like the idea of a knife cutting into my throat. I'd finally found my voice. I was not about to put it in harm's way.

Twenty years later, after numerous traditional and nontraditional interventions, the swelling on the right side of my throat was so large, I agreed it was time to remove it. While there are any number of physical causes for this—genetics, diet, endocrine disrupters—there are also more subtle nonphysical ones.

Our voice is a living presence inside us. Our voice is us. The thyroid sits on top of its exit gate. When the thyroid is in balance, it does its job of regulating the endocrine system and leaves everything else alone. In my case, however, the thyroid had grown into a bloated blob that was blocking the gateway of my voice. Remember the woman who asked me why I was hiding? Perhaps it wasn't me who was hiding. Perhaps my bloated thyroid was hiding me.

The body is the record keeper of our life. Everything that happens to us is stored there, along with all the emotional material we feel or repress. All of this weaves into the psycho-emotional wounds, conscious and unconscious, we carry inside ourselves. When we view the body through the lens of masculine and feminine categories, the right side is considered of the masculine, and the left of the feminine. So looking through this lens, we could say my thyroid was a physical manifestation of an amped-up patriarchal masculine that was not only overpowering its feminine half, it was attempting to obliterate, i.e., suffocate, me.

To See and Be Seen

I am the daughter of a narcissistic mother. This is not a critique against her. Her narcissism was not her. It was a complex tapestry of grandiosity and repression, a defense against the pain and trauma of her own life. She did her best. She really did. It's just that she was blinded by her inability to see my sister and me as we actually were. When she looked at us, all she saw was herself. Anything she saw that was not like her was critiqued, dismissed, competed with, or rejected. Any longing we had, any dream that might take us beyond her, was undermined.

Every child needs to be seen and embraced as the person they actually are. This is the greatest gift a parent or caregiver, and later on, our teachers and role models, can give. In their seeing, we learn to see ourselves. Without this seeing, we are prey to the wounding/wounded masculine's twisted power games.

I have worked with many daughters of narcissistic mothers. I have also worked with many sons. We all share variations of a common theme: a sense that we are always at risk of obliteration and therefore need to hide. Our hiding takes many forms. We may seem visible to others. We may seem self-actualized. As we dig below the surface, however, we find a wounded girl- or boy-child hiding in the underground.

Since we tend to project the dynamic of our relationship with our mother onto the world, it stays with us long after we've left home. I fought hard against the wound of my mother's obliteration. In the end, I won. Perhaps I am stronger for it. Nevertheless, it's not a path I wish on anyone.

There's a specific category of mantras that are called bija mantras. These are considered seed forms of the archetypal fields. In the same way that the acorn seeds the oak tree, the bija mantras seed the archetypal potentials within us. Saraswatī's bija mantra is transliterated as the word "aim." We don't pronounce it in the English way, however. We pronounce it as "iim" as in "I'm," the contraction of "I am." So as English speakers, we get a double whammy. When we sing or chant Saraswatī's bija mantra, we're not only invoking a sense of self that transcends language, we're also receiving a literal boost through our association with these two words and their meaning.

I am.

Take a moment and feel your voice as it lives inside you. Trace the path of its flow. And listen. Really listen. Perhaps you'll hear it whispering "IamIamIamIam . . ."

Have I told you that Saraswatī has a sense of humor? When I began putting this chapter together, I thought I'd start by copying and pasting from all the Saraswatī articles I've written. There's a lot of excellent material there. But I just couldn't make it work. It all struck me as yesterday's news. That's when I realized I had to start with a blank page. That's when I heard her laughing.

om srī saraswatī mā

Standing in the Ground of I Am

Saraswatī is associated with the color white. This whiteness is attributed to aesthetic and intellectual purity, a simplistic and superficial, not to mention racist, understanding I bought into for many years. No. Saraswatī is the blank page, the blank canvas, the empty stage. Binary values of pure and impure or black and white have nothing to do with it.

The blank page is a mystery, a background that gives no cover. There is nowhere to hide. It beckons us into its blankness. It beckons us to say something, write something, draw something, become something. And then, to stand by what we have made and say, "I am."

I am.

Much of the messaging we receive in our lives is about all that we are not. "I'm not smart enough, beautiful enough, handsome enough, fit enough, strong enough, successful enough, wealthy enough, happy enough, athletic enough, artistic enough, working enough, relaxing enough, exercising enough, studying enough, sleeping enough, healthy enough . . ."

It really does get tedious.

Here's the truth, plain and simple. We are human beings bumbling along, each one an ongoing work in progress. It's not about being perfect specimens in an external validation game. The dirty secret of this game is we'll never be enough. In fact, not being enough is what keeps this game going. You have to ask yourself, "Why am I playing such a stupid game?"

I am and that is enough.

The Dharma of Speech

The aspect of Saraswatī you might think of as her skeletal system is often referred to as the *dharma of speech*: speak only that which is kind, true, necessary, and at the appropriate time. To this we add, do only that which is kind, true, necessary, and at the appropriate time. And think only that which is kind, true, necessary, and at the appropriate time. Practicing the dharma of speech is one of Saraswatī's great secrets. Thirteen words that can change your life.

> Speak only that which is kind, true, necessary, and at the appropriate time.

I want to pause for a moment to reflect on silence. Sit back in your chair. Close your eyes. And ride your breath into the space inside you. Draw it in. Breathe it out. Gently. Ever so gently. Slowly. Ever so slowly. Stretch out your breath until it seems as if it could last forever.

om srī saraswatī mā

The Four Levels of Sound

Silence is the origin place. Everything that is begins here. In Mantra Yoga, we map out the sonic path—it's called the four levels of sound—our voice will follow, from its origin point of silence to its out-of-the-mouth expression. A lot happens to our voice as it moves through the gates of this path.

Imagine a channel running through the center of your being. If it's free of the obstructing, obliterating, ominous omniscience of a wounding masculine, your voice will rise from the ground of silence—we call this the *para* level—and move into the belly. This is the *pashyanti* level. Here, your voice will be nourished and shaped by intuition, insight, knowledge, and wisdom, preparing it to move closer to felt awareness before it enters the *madhyama* level at the heart. Here it will be checked for kindness, truth, necessity, and appropriateness before it moves into the *vaikhari* level at the mouth, where it becomes spoken words or thought thoughts.

This is the channel of our voice. This is the space where Saraswatī resides. I leave you to imagine how your voice is defamed, denied, devalued, deprived, distorted, dismembered, derided, disdained, co-opted, gaslit, shamed, or silenced, when its sonic pathway is controlled by the wounding masculine.

We want to reclaim this pathway, to clear the debris of interior voices that are not our voice. I'm talking about those interior voices that may pretend to be us, but all they want is to shut us down.

om srī saraswatī mā

So many times in my life I was made wrong by others. So many times I knew that I was not wrong. The problem was I didn't have the language to defend myself, so I retreated to my lonely corner. As I began to find my voice, I realized no defense was necessary. It was enough to say something like, "I can't find the words for what I'd like to say right now, but I'll tell you this: I'm not wrong." And if I wasn't yet ready to speak this out loud, it was enough to speak it to myself.

I have noticed that much of what passes for conversation is a kind of one-upmanship exchange of gossip, opinion, and projection, or a toxic discharge of anger and anxiety. Rather than openhearted listening, where we actually take in what another is saying and respond to that, many of us are on autopilot, barely paying attention, self-referencing, or thinking about what we'll say before our conversation partner has even finished speaking. This is not conversation. This is monologue.

> Speak only that which is kind, true, necessary, and at the appropriate time . . .

So much talk is driven by the need to be right and also, by our fear of silence. We've been shamed into caring more about how we're perceived, into letting no one see our vulnerabilities, into avoiding the discomfort of being wrong, into keeping the conversation going, that we lose touch with the powerful stance of listening, and of simply being as we are.

I am and that is more than enough.

We don't have to know everything. We don't have to be finished. We certainly don't have to be right. All we have to do is listen and rest in our light. All we have to do is think, speak, and live that which is kind, true, necessary, and at the appropriate time. All we have to do is remember that every time we stand in this ground, we can be sure that Kālī and Lakṣmī are cheering from the sidelines and Saraswatī is dancing through the house.

om srī saraswatī mā

Chapter 12

KUAN YIN

The mysterious sound of Kuan Yin's name
is holy like the ocean's thunder . . .
call upon it never doubting,
a never-wavering support . . .
—The Lotus Sutra

Here's what you need to know about Kuan Yin. Her full name is Kuan Shih Yin, which translates as "She Who Hears the Cries of the World." Most people refer to her without the "Shih." Depending upon the system of transliteration, you'll see her name spelled as Kuan Yin, Kuan-Yin, Quan Yin, Guan-Yin, Guan Yin, or Guanyin. In Japan, she's called Kannon; in Tibet, Chenrezig. She has profound connections with Mary, the Mother of Jesus, as well as the goddess Tara. In some ways, the three are one. They share the same archetypal DNA.

Kuan Yin has a complex lineage. In popular versions of her story, she begins life as Miao Shan, the youngest daughter of an autocratic king who cannot deal with the fact that his child's values—he wants her to be a proper princess, marry a proper prince, and produce proper heirs, while she wants to leave the court, never marry, and follow a monastic path—are different from his own. Desperate to force her to his will, he punishes and torments her for years. When all his attempts fail, he sentences her to death. In the end he gets his due and she, well, she becomes Kuan Yin.

In scholarly circles, Kuan Yin begins life in India as the masculine bodhisattva called Avalokiteśvara. Within the Buddhist tradition, the bodhisattva is considered an embodiment of compassion, someone who chooses to defer his or her enlightenment until there is no more suffering on the earth. In other words, choosing to stick around rather than being released from what Buddhists call samsara and the rest of us call daily life.

Within Buddhism, Avalokiteśvara is the Man, an extraordinarily powerful, revered, and beloved bodhisattva. By the time he reaches China, he's morphed into Kuan Yin, making them perhaps the most famous and beloved transgender being of all time.

om śrī kuan yin mā

The Mysteries of the Heart

There's a wealth of wisdom contained within the English translation of Kuan Yin's name: She Who Hears the Cries of the World. This is a name formed in the mysteries of the heart. Look at the five letters of the word "heart."

H E A R T

The word "hear" makes up the first four letters. And in the middle, between *h* and *t*, you can see the word "ear." It's all spelled out right there. Without hearing, there is no heart. And the ear sits at the center of the heart.

Most every wisdom tradition I've encountered holds the heart as a central metaphor. In Tantric Hindu and Buddhist circles, we speak of the heart chakra, the subtle energy portal at the center of the chest. This chakra, whose Sanskrit name is anahata, is formed and re-formed as we move through our lives. It holds impressions of all we experience and becomes a template for how we relate to ourselves and the world. It may grow wider and brighter over the years, emanating a luminosity that makes everyone and everything around us feel better. It can also go the other way, closing us off, shutting us down, hardening into the heaviness that breeds cruelty, hostility, and the need to control. One of the first doors the wounded heart closes is the door to the ears. When we live under its influence, we're unable to listen or to hear.

To see the truth, to live in truth, requires deep listening. The kind of listening that actually hears; the kind of listening that reaches out from itself so that it sees, truly sees, the other—whether that other is a tree, rock, enemy, lover, or the voice of our own heart. This is the essence of Kuan Yin.

In my guru's Upstate New York ashram, there was a temple in the gardens built around a life-size statue of his guru. There were alcoves in the walls, each one holding a statue of a Hindu deity, and standing near the entryway, an exquisite rendering of Kuan Yin. She was nearly five feet tall and carved of white marble. I loved that statue. I could gaze at it for hours. Little did I suspect that one day, Kuan Yin would play a role in my leaving the guru.

The Renaissance of the Sacred Feminine

It was February 1994 when I first heard about the conference. It was called the Renaissance of the Sacred Feminine, and would be held in San Francisco in early June. Although I felt a strong pull to attend, the logistics were tricky and the cost substantial, so I spent the next couple of months ignoring the pull. By May, every cell in my body was screaming that I had to go. A few weeks later I was on a plane heading into SFO.

From the moment I arrived, however, something was off. The Renaissance of the Sacred Feminine seemed more about male ego than feminine renaissance, and I wandered around for the first couple of days trying to figure out why in goddess's name I'd spent a small fortune and flown across the country to be here.

The first tiny clue came on Saturday afternoon when I ran into an old ashram friend. We hadn't seen each other in a while and were joyously catching up when the conversation turned to ashram news. She grew reticent, mumbled something about keeping her distance, and suddenly had to go. It was a strange moment, par for the course of this strange conference, however, and I walked on, continuing my search for clues about why I'd felt so compelled to come.

By 5:00 p.m. that day I was done, ready to pack my bags and leave. And then, there it was, the quietest inner impulse, nudging me to walk down to a nearby restaurant for dinner. When I got there, the place was packed with conference attendees. There was one other single woman waiting to be seated, and the hostess asked if we'd mind sharing a table. Which is how I ended up having one of the most important conversations of my life with a total stranger.

As it turned out, our lives had many intersecting points, and we talked nonstop for a couple of hours. Somewhere in our long conversation, she mentioned she'd heard there was a scandal brewing in my ashram community and wondered if I knew anything about it. To me, this seemed unlikely. I said it was probably a handful of disgruntled devotees spreading rumors, and our conversation moved on.

She needed to return to the conference before me, so I walked back alone. As I made my way up the hill, there it was again, this time much louder, this time every cell in my body shouting, "This is why you had to come to this conference. You had to meet this woman. You had to have this conversation."

The next day it all came clear. I ran into my old friend again and asked if she'd heard anything about an ashram scandal. She looked at me intently. "Do you really want to know?" she asked. "Yes!" I said. "What is going on?"

It was a beautiful morning. We were standing in the garden courtyard of the conference center, people milling around us as we talked. She told me a tale of sexual and emotional abuse in our guru's inner circle. I so wanted not to believe a word. But it all rang true. Too many dots connected to pretend there was no there there. Listening, I felt the belief system I'd lived inside of for nearly two decades begin to shatter.

She got to the end of the story, and the next thing I knew, I felt a lightning bolt of energy come blasting into me, right into my heart chakra. It was so potent I had a sense of falling backward. Then the courtyard where we were talking disappeared, my friend disappeared, and I was tumbling down, down, down. When I landed, I found myself sitting in the lap of a larger-than-life female being who I realized was Kuan Yin. Eyes twinkling, laughter in her voice, she looked at me sweetly and said, "What took you so long?!"

om śrī kuan yin mā

I sat there dazed for a moment, mostly in wonder. Then everything shifted and I was back in the courtyard again, standing with my friend. She looked at me quizzically. Clearly something profound had just happened. "Yes," I said. "I guess it's over. I guess I'm done."

This was the shattering—as I later came to understand it—of the projection of my own spiritual authority, the innate power I'd projected onto the guru for so many years. It was also the moment when my relationship with Kuan Yin shifted from one that was mostly aesthetic to something way deeper and profound. This was a get-down-dirty, in my face—well actually, in her lap—experience that brought me smack-dab into the living reality of this archetypal presence that was quite clearly inside me. All those years of projecting it outward. Why did it take me so long?!

Well, we know the answer to that one. We're formed in a system that undermines the wisdom of the belly and the heart. We're bred to give our power away, to outsource it to that outside person, authority, whoever, whatever, we're trained to believe knows better than we do. This is what keeps the system going. It wants us blind, deaf, and mute. Which makes listening to oneself an act of courage. Which makes walking the path of heart a warrior's path. Which puts us at risk when we question the people or institutions that have claimed our allegiance.

Becoming Kuan Yin

I'm going to tell you the story of Miao Shan's transformation into Kuan Yin. Like all the great stories, this one unfolds on many levels. We can read it as a heroine's journey with a happy ending and leave it at that. If we want to peer more deeply into it, we can see Miao Shan as a mirror of our most exalted self, and her father as a mirror of the wounding/wounded masculine's compulsion to keep us from fully embodying that self. At the macro level, Miao Shan is a metaphor for the earth. Viewed through this lens, her father is a metaphor for the patriarchal assault on our planet. And if we choose to read between the lines, we can find the story of the transformation of the patriarch.

Rather than give a brief synopsis like those I wrote in previous chapters, I'm giving you a long-form version. So settle back, enter into this story, and see yourself between its lines . . .

Miao Shan was the third daughter of an autocratic king who expected all his daughters to marry, produce heirs, and live out their lives in the luxury of the court. After Miao Shan's sisters were successfully wed, their father began to plan her betrothal. When he called her to him, to tell her which prince he'd selected, she bowed her head and said, "Father, I cannot marry. My only wish is to attain the Pure Heart Mind of Buddhahood."

This enraged the king. He could not abide anyone, even his beloved young daughter, saying no to his command. "You dare defy my wishes," he exclaimed. "Go to the forest then. And do not return until you have realized the folly of your ways." After a time, he sent her sisters to find her, assuming she'd be cold, hungry, and desperate to return. Instead, they found her living peacefully among a family of wolves.

Her sisters begged Miao Shan to come home. "I will return," she said, "but I cannot marry. I will ask our father to allow me to enter the Nunnery of the White Bird."

The king was secretly delighted to see Miao Shan. She was, after all, his favorite daughter. So he agreed to her request, instructing the abbess to assign the young princess chores that would break her.

Terrified to go against this king, the abbess gave Miao Shan the most difficult work in the abbey, sending her out through the long, cold nights to patrol the nunnery gates, and then at sunrise, into the kitchens to prepare all the meals for her sister nuns. The hours were long, the work exhausting, but Miao Shan never faltered or complained.

Throughout this time, the Master of Heaven was watching. Moved by Miao Shan's forbearance, he called on the North Star, saying, "Find the wolves who sheltered Miao Shan in the forest. Send them to her. Let them guard the gates. Then find a family of birds to help her in the kitchen and send those to her too." Miao Shan received her animal friends with great affection and all lived happily within the nunnery walls.

When the king next spoke with the abbess, expecting her to tell him how Miao Shan suffered, the abbess said, "My king, I have done as you commanded, but your daughter thrives. And miracles are happening around her." Upon hearing this, the king grew so incensed, he ordered his army to surround the nunnery and burn it to the ground.

Standing outside as flames engulfed the building, Miao Shan offered a prayer to the Master of Heaven, asking that her sister nuns be saved. Then, taking a pin from her hair, she pricked the roof of her mouth and spat out several drops of blood. The drops floated into the sky, where they became huge dark clouds, and then a drenching rain poured down, extinguishing all the fires.

Now the king was livid. "No one defies me," he shouted, "certainly not my youngest daughter." Then he called the captain of the palace guard and said, "Arrest her and bring her to me." When Miao Shan was brought to his chambers, he gave her an ultimatum: "Repent your disobedient ways, Miao Shan, or you will die."

For Miao Shan, there was no choice. She looked at him with great sadness and said, "Honored Father, I can no more turn from my calling than ask the moon to leave the sky. If you desire to take my life for this, so be it."

Once again, the Master of Heaven was listening. Once again, he called on the North Star. "Attend Miao Shan's execution," he instructed, "and be sure she suffers no pain. Then change into a tiger and whisk her away before she breathes her last breath. Take great care to preserve her body. Let no harm come to her."

On the day of Miao Shan's execution, the sky was dark. Yet the moment she placed her head on the block, a golden light surrounded her. The executioner raised his sword. As it touched her neck, however, the blade shattered. Then the king sent two guardsmen to stab her. But their spears disintegrated as they raised them. Finally, he commanded the executioner to strangle her with a silken cord.

As Miao Shan was taking her final breath, the tiger appeared. Whisking away her physical body, he stood guard as her spirit body journeyed through the underworld. Moving among the suffering souls there, she offered kindness and comfort to all. As she heard their cries, the stale air grew fresh, the darkness turned to light, and their wails of anguish became songs of joy. This was the moment when Miao Shan found her true name: She Who Hears the Cries of the World.

Now she returned to the above world where the tiger sat guarding her physical form. Reentering her body, she was greeted by the Buddha of the West, who offered her a golden peach and said, "This is the peach of immortality. Eat it very slowly. With each bite you will merge more fully into its light." Then the Buddha bowed and disappeared.

The next thing she knew, Miao Shan, who was now Kuan Yin, was transported to an old monastery on the island of Potala. She lived there for nine years, ministering to the old and infirm, to the sailors and their families, to anyone who called for her aid.

Back at the palace, the king was not well. Besieged by an illness that covered his body with pus-filled sores, he lived in a fog of torment and pain. The court physicians and healers tried every remedy, but nothing worked. Desperate for relief, he issued an edict, proclaiming, "Whoever can cure me will become my heir." Healers, physicians, and holy men came from all over the kingdom. No matter what remedy or incantation they offered, however, none could heal this king.

Learning of her father's suffering, Kuan Yin traveled to his court, disguised as a humble priest. When she reached the palace gates, she told the guards, "I have heard of the king's illness. I can prepare a medicine that will cure him." She was immediately admitted to his chamber. Coming into his royal bedroom, she kneeled before him, explaining, "I can make an ointment, my lord, that will restore your health. I simply need your men to procure two special ingredients. Someone who loves you must offer their arm and their eye. Once you have obtained these two, I will return and prepare the healing salve." So word went out through the kingdom, but to no avail. No one loved this king enough to offer arm or eye.

Sensing her father was close to death, Kuan Yin returned to the palace, still disguised as the humble priest. Once again, the guardsmen brought her to his bedchamber. This time her mother and sisters sat beside him. All three were weeping. Through their tears they whispered, "Alas, kind sir, we have failed. No one in this kingdom will offer our king their arm or eye."

And then he, who was really She, gazed at them with great tenderness and said, "Then you must call the head guard to me now. Tell him to bring a golden bowl and very sharp sword." When the guard appeared, the disguised priest held out an arm and said, "Take it off and place it in this bowl."

The shocked guard did as he was told. Then the priest pulled his own eye out of its socket. Placing it in the bowl with his arm, he prepared the ointment, then gently rubbed it into all the sores on the king's body. Immediately, the king was healed.

Climbing from his sickbed, the king bowed to the priest and said, "I offer you the honor of my vow. You will be my heir." The priest bowed back to the king, and with gentle laughter, assumed her true form as Kuan Yin, and disappeared.

Everyone had been so intent on the humble priest's dramatic actions, no one noticed the queen had fainted when his arm was cut. Now, as she regained consciousness, she told them she would recognize that arm anywhere and said, "This was no priest. This was the princess Miao Shan, who has become everything she longed to be and more." Then they all fell to the ground, weeping in joy and something deeper and more profound, weeping with the wisdom of remorse. And on the very next morning, they traveled to Potala, and gathering around Miao Shan who was now Kuan Yin, devoted themselves to living lives of compassion and loving-kindness for all.

om śrī kuan yin mā

If She Can Do It, So Can We

Of all the goddess archetypes we're looking at in this book, Miao Shan is the only one who begins life as human. In other words, if she can do it, so can we. So let's not buy into the superhuman superhero myth imposed upon her.

Let's see ourselves in her story. Let's look deeply into this mirror of father and daughter and Father and the World. Let's feel the joy of Miao Shan's transcendence, but not gloss over the agony, rage, and despair that got her there. Let's not sugarcoat this most essential journey with magic and miracles. Healing, transformation, and reclamation do not come easy. Let's not cheapen Miao Shan's (or ours or the planet's) with flashy parlor tricks.

Let's also think about the narrative arc of Miao Shan's father. His story tends to be subsumed in his daughter's. And while we can celebrate Miao Shan's transformation into Kuan Yin, what is never alluded to in the traditional tellings is that in order to fully embody her Kuan Yin possibility, Miao Shan has to return to the palace and heal her father. Without this act, the story is incomplete. The fact is, his transformation is as important as hers.

Reclaiming the Sacred Masculine

We live in the debris of six thousand years of patriarchal annihilation of everything that's stood in its way. The patriarchal mindset has literally broken the ecosystem of the earth. During my lifetime we've gone from talk of global warming, to shouts of climate crisis, to screams of climate catastrophe. And still, shockingly, the unsustainable beat goes on.

Bringing our planet back from this nightmare requires all hands on deck. And this requires we get really serious about transforming everything embedded and embodied in the paradigm of the patriarchal masculine. Including the myth of the superhuman superhero.

We don't need superheroes. We don't have time to wait for a magical savior who doesn't exist and will never come. The sacred masculine has got to reclaim its power from the psychopathic patriarch. And as I've said over and over again: The sacred feminine, goddess, being—call *it* whatever you like—is the medicine. Because it—sacred feminine, goddess, being—is the power that must be reclaimed.

For us, living at this pivotal moment in Earth's history, this is what Kuan Yin's story is most pointedly about: reclamation of a vibrant, vital feminine to restore a lovingly engaged masculine. Right here, right now, "being" and "doing" working in a perfect union of compassion and love. This is the ultimate work of the goddess: to rise up, and in that arising, to shatter the shackles that have trapped the true masculine in six thousand years of patriarchal strangulation. Within this shattering sits the awesome possibility of healing ourselves and the world.

> For us, living at this pivotal moment in Earth's history, this is what Kuan Yin's story is most pointedly about: reclamation of a vibrant, vital feminine to restore a lovingly engaged masculine. Right here, right now, "being" and "doing" working in a perfect union of compassion and love. This is the ultimate work of the goddess: to rise up, and in that arising, to shatter the shackles that have trapped the true masculine in six thousand years of patriarchal strangulation. Within this shattering sits the awesome possibility of healing ourselves and the world.

My Father and Me

Twenty years before he died, my father and I had a major rupture in our relationship. The catalyst was a phone call with my mom when I was melting down over an IRS bill. For her, a woman still traumatized by growing up during the Great Depression, the threat of financial insecurity could send her over the edge. I wasn't in crisis, just momentarily upset—and alas, not wise enough to keep it to myself.

This sent her into a panic. Without checking with me, she called my dad (they were no longer living together), telling him I was in financial trouble (I was not) and imploring him to send me money. This enraged him. He had zero tolerance for her panics and even less for women wanting money from him. (Much later, I discovered he'd had, to put it delicately, a couple of opportunistic girlfriends hitting him up for cash.) Rather than calling to find out what was going on with me, I received an angry, rant-filled letter filled with bitter accusations that I was a profligate masquerading as an artist and spiritual seeker. It was an awful thing to receive from anyone. Receiving it from my father was devastating.

I was still years away from learning the carefully guarded secret of his "prison years" and of understanding the shame and guilt that secret cost him. I was, however, beginning to face the fact that the charismatic father I'd idealized since childhood had a dark side. Throughout my life I'd overheard snatches of conversations that hinted at his cruelty. This was the first time I was the target.

I sat with that letter for several weeks, examining myself through the lens of his perceptions. Was there truth there? Did I have blinders on? In the end I wrote a long, thoughtful response, carefully addressing his allegations. His wrote back two lines: *Got your letter. You're a good writer.*

If letter number 1 had hurt me, letter number 2 really ticked me off. I was still too young in my journey to understand that this was the best he could do. Had I been able to forgive him, had he been able to apologize, the whole thing would have blown over. Instead, we had no contact for close to a decade. When I learned through the family grapevine that he was cutting me out of his will, I was not surprised.

I'd done a lot of growing during those years. I was much stronger in my sense of self and way more adept at navigating the complexities of daily life. Nevertheless, I was not ready to forgive him. So much time had passed with no contact, it was like he no longer existed. Like we were dead to each other. Then my sister called to tell me he'd had a heart attack, and I realized I'd been dreading that call for my entire life and had to go see him.

He'd left New York after retiring, drawn to the sunshine and poker tables of Las Vegas. My sister and I met at the airport and made our way to his apartment complex. I still remember standing at the front door as we rang the bell. I was feeling some trepidation, but there was no turning back. I'll never know what he experienced when he saw me. Upon seeing him, however, my anxiety was replaced by shock. The man greeting us in that open doorway was a shadow of the father I'd known. He'd been a tall man, strong and sure, with an easy grace and quiet good looks. Now he was shrinking into himself, so weak he had to lean against the wall for support.

He beckoned us in and we sat down in the living room. After a few moments of awkward silence, my sister got up to make tea. As soon as we were alone, he turned to me and asked why I'd come, telling me I would get no money from him, going on about what a disappointment I was, that my life in the arts was frivolous, that my meditation practice was a waste of time, and just to be sure I got it, telling me he'd cut me out of his will.

I sat there for a moment, stunned by the force of rage coming from this man so diminished that he could barely stand on his own. When it was clear he was done, I told him that I'd come because he'd had a heart attack and I was his daughter. As far as his money was concerned, I had no claim on it. At this point my sister came back into the room and the three of us made small talk for a few minutes. Then he started in with me again. Same accusations, dialed up a few notches. There was nothing to do but sit quietly and repeat what I'd already said. That I had not come for his money. That I had come to help care for him. That I was not leaving until I saw he was strong enough to be on his own. By now I was over any trepidation and awkwardness. If he wanted to bicker with me, so be it. But we had work to do. The apartment was a mess. There was no food in the refrigerator. And he needed to get back to bed.

Over the next two days, my sister and I cleaned the apartment until it sparkled, filling it with fresh flowers, stocking the refrigerator with healthy food, preparing lovely home-cooked meals, baking his favorite pies, and turning his dank patio into a serene oasis. All of this in between tending to his every need. I won't say it was warm between us, but we'd shifted into a kind of détente.

By the third day my sister decided to give us space and began leaving us alone in the apartment. This was when he started telling me stories from his life. Although he wasn't ready to reveal his big secret—I didn't discover that until later—he talked about his father's death when he was five years old, about his immigrant mother having to raise six children on her own. He told me about having to drop out of school in the sixth grade to help support the family, about living on the street as a young man during the Great Depression, "eating dirt," as he said, and dreaming of driving an ice cream truck so he could pull over to the side of the road and eat a whole tub of the stuff. He spoke of meeting my mom, moving to Los Angeles, coming back to New York to build the business. He talked, I listened. He talked, I listened. The days passed. He grew stronger, the space between us softer.

Toward the end of our time together, he started talking about death. Before our decade-long rupture, we often talked metaphysics and philosophy. This was different. This was not intellectual. This was heart to heart. It seemed to me that he was trying to prepare.

And then he asked me to teach him how to meditate . . .

I can still see him sitting there. Closing his eyes, following his breath, repeating the mantra I taught him. And there we were, after all the awfulness that had passed between us, sitting together in the big space of Being, the big space of the Heart. No words, apologies, or acknowledgments of hurts and misunderstandings necessary. It was the silence of listening that opened the closed doors between us. The listening that hears the cries of the world. This is the secret of Kuan Yin. It's all about the listening that actually hears. Talk is cheap. Listening is the currency of love.

om srī kuan yin mā

The Currency of Love

One of the many ironies of the patriarchal mind is the way it twists ideals of forgiveness and compassion. We're told to turn the other cheek, to forgive and forget. But these often require us to shut down, turn off, and tune out. I've worked with many people who are certain they've forgiven those who've hurt them. Too often, however, we confuse forgiveness with splitting off from the hurt, pain, or anger, the hatred and shock, the traumas we still hold in our bodies. True forgiveness requires us to face into all of this and to listen, really listen, to its voice.

This is what Miao Shan is doing when she journeys to the underworld. Like her, we need to hear the cries of all the stuff we've buried deep inside ourselves. Otherwise the patriarchal masculine will weaponize our pain and hurt and anger against us, and we'll end up with symptoms like headaches, stomachaches, immune disorders, eczema, insomnia, depression, and anxiety.

Which is not to say there's no physical component or genetics in these ailments. Simply to say that when we unpack them, we often find a wounding/wounded masculine twisting us up, tying our hands behind our back, stuffing a gag into our mouth, and aiming its toxic messaging arrows at the bull's-eye centers of belly, throat, heart, and mind.

Miao Shan's father is a study in not listening. He's a man who cannot hear, a man so lost in his notion of the way things should be, he's blind to the way they actually are. In order to wake him up, he needs to be brought to his knees. First by a crippling illness. Second by the shock that no one loves him enough to offer an eye or an arm. Third by the realization that the miraculous healer who does is none other than the daughter he so cruelly abused.

Kuan Yin's eye and arm represent clear seeing and embodied compassion. In order for the king to heal, these two must awaken (or be force-fed) into him. The story makes it very clear: The patriarch must be brought to his (or her) knees. The patriarch must face into its cruelty and lies. The patriarch must surrender to the luminous power of the deep feminine.

Kuan Yin is often portrayed as a princess turned bodhisattva who bestows no-questions-asked compassion to all. This fosters a false notion of what compassion actually is. Saccharine-sweet docility is not part of the program.

True compassion walks hand in hand with clear seeing. We don't have one without the other. Without clear seeing, we're incapable of hearing the cries of the world. To see into the nature of things with no fantasy and/or projection is to see (and hear) life as it actually is. No dissociation. No attachment to story or belief system. Pricking one's mouth to draw blood, cutting off one's arm, pulling out one's eye, these are metaphors for turning full-faced into whatever is arising. There's a fierceness to it. This is action determined to set ourselves and the world right again. This is truth come crashing into the room. And truth is the blood of compassion.

The force field of Kālī is very much present in the compassion of Kuan Yin. And like her sister Kālī, Kuan Yin requires no thanks for her service. Yet there is always a price. The spell of the patriarch will be broken. The sacred masculine will rise from its ashes. And love will stand in that place.

om srī kuan yin mā

Chapter 13

BEFORE WE MOVE FORWARD, A QUICK REVIEW

I have to see a thing a thousand times
before I see it once.
—Thomas Wolfe

As I've said throughout this book, the patriarchal paradigm destroying our planet also lives within our mind/body system as the voice of the inner patriarch or wounding/wounded, aka broken, masculine. This psychic distortion has been deforming the true masculine for thousands of years, forcing it to dissociate from the feminine ground. This denial of its other half fosters patriarchy in all its brutal, dissociative forms.

Needless to say, warming weather, ramped-up species extinction, massive droughts, storms, wildfires, and melting ice caps, not to mention endless war, forced migration, starvation, poverty, and a crew of grifters and autocrats posing as corporate and political leaders does not bode well for planet Earth.

Lest anyone still reading thinks that by patriarchy I'm referring only to men, let me be clear that while the aforementioned crew of grifters and autocrats has historically been composed mostly of men, there are growing numbers of women (and nonbinaries) among its ranks. Patriarchy is not an illness confined to people of the male gender. An equal-opportunity virus, it rots the minds of everyone.

> Patriarchy is not an illness confined to people of the male gender. An equal-opportunity virus, it rots the minds of everyone.

Some believe it all has to shatter before a new order can form. Others think it's more about tweaking a broken system. Still others have simply tuned out. I'm all for shattering, rebuilding, revisioning, and repairing. I just think this work has to happen inside of ourselves, parallel to and concurrent with our outer work in the world.

I've not written off activism and movement building. I just don't trust anyone's revolutionary program if they haven't logged in at least a decade of integrated inner work. Patriarchy is genius at recreating itself. I see way too much unconscious motivation, way too much projection, displacement, egoic grandiosity, and identity-driven everything to leave me feeling comfortable with Left, Right, or Center. As for tuning out, I'm afraid that option is off the table. We have got to seriously tune in.

I started writing this book in early 2019. Here in America we were a year out from the arrival of COVID and two years out from the apocalyptic trifecta of wildfires, superstorms, and brutal heat waves that even climate change deniers could no longer deny. During the six years I worked on this book, I watched the America I thought I knew—a country doing egregious things around the world and ignoring serious problems here at home, yet somehow remaining predictably banal—become awash with hatred for the "other," with militias armed with assault weapons springing up like weeds, with "open carry" laws adopted by state after state, with conspiracy theories going mainstream, and a Supreme Court inspired more by *The Handmaid's Tale* than the US Constitution.

While there are bright spots on the horizon, it is, overall, a terrifying picture. We are living in patriarchy on steroids, making it more incumbent than ever on people like you and me, people who have the luxury to read a book like this one, to take the work of world-mending, inner and outer, very seriously. At best, this will help turn the tide. At least, it will fuel the inner strength we need to navigate these times.

One of the patriarchal mindset's favored ways of demeaning inner work is to refer to it with that most derogatory phrase, "navel-gazing." Note to self: Always be suspicious of anything this mindset belittles. The odds are, it feels a threat to its hegemony.

Turning within is an act of power that opens the gates to seeing the world as it actually is: All One. We are each other's keepers, utterly and inalterably connected and interdependent. Nothing terrifies the patriarch more than this awareness. Because once we realize the ineffable fact of our interconnectedness, we have eliminated its favored weapon: divide and conquer.

> When someone works for less pay than she can live on—when, for example, she goes hungry so that you can eat more cheaply and conveniently—then she has made a great sacrifice for you, she has made you a gift of some part of her abilities, her health, and her life. The "working poor," as they are approvingly termed, are in fact the major philanthropists of our society. They neglect their own children so that the children of others will be cared for; they live in substandard housing so that other homes will be shiny and perfect; they endure privation so that inflation will be low and stock prices high. To be a member of the working poor is to be an anonymous donor, a nameless benefactor, to everyone else.
>
> —*Barbara Ehrenreich*

> Relationships are all there is. Everything in the universe only exists because it is in relationship to everything else. Nothing exists in isolation. We have to stop pretending we are individuals that can go it alone.
> —*Margaret J. Wheatley*

In Parts I and II of this book, I broke down what is essentially a seamless whole. This required the dualistic framing of concepts like doing and being, masculine and feminine, god and goddess. Now, as we move into Part III, we can begin letting go of this framing, resting in the whole that is so much greater than the sum of its parts. I would like to never again use that most annoying word "patriarchy." I'm as sick of writing it as you must be of reading it. Before we move forward, however, a quick review . . .

The (Masculine) Container Is Where (Feminine) Being Happens

Everything happens within the container of the masculine. The infrastructure that drives our doing function, the container is the "I" of "I am." It's what gets us out of bed in the morning, holds us through our day, and moves us through every action in our lives. All of it—every thought, written, spoken, or silent; every decision, assumption, perception, projection; every act we do, think about doing, avoid doing, or choose not to do—happens through the masculine container.

The feminine is the ground of being. It's the "am" of "I am," that is expressed or silenced, supported or attacked, cherished or obliterated, through the doing functions of thinking, speaking, and acting. The doing function is attuned to whatever is arising from the inner ground. In a healthy system, it grabs hold of an impulse, makes a yes/no evaluation, and based on that, offers the containing needed to make the impulse happen, or suggests we let this one go. In a wounding/wounded system, the doing function is corrupted by the patriarchal masculine.

Patriarchal, aka Wounding/Wounded or Broken, Masculine

The patriarchal masculine is a distortion of the doing function. As it develops, it fills the mind/body system with false narratives about who and what we are. Its messaging, delivered mostly through the inner voices of our self-talk, tends to be critical, shaming, destructive, delusional, or grandiose. Under its influence, we come to believe its voices are our own. The patriarchal masculine's presence in our mind is the ultimate form of identity theft. It steals our sense of self. Ironically, although it seems powerful, it's actually a broken function, desperately in need of the balance that only a strong feminine offers.

> The patriarchal masculine's presence in our mind is the ultimate form of identity theft. It steals our sense of self.

The Wounded Feminine

When being is suppressed by the patriarchal masculine, it's forced into tiny cracks and crevices in the psyche, where it shrivels and wanes, its power stolen and weaponized against us. This internal imbalance often leads to anxiety, depression, and inflammatory illness. When feminine being is suffocated by an overgrown masculine, it can't provide the counterbalance necessary for a healthy system.

The Integration of Being and Doing

Being needs the shaping facility of doing. Doing needs the energy and power, the consciousness, of being. One without the other is dangerous. Too much being and we drown in the waters of the unconscious. Too much doing and we lose connection to the truth of who and what we are. We want these primary aspects of our human being-ness to nest in a harmony of perfect integration. This integration is the foundation of living wise, living joyous, living free.

> If we are ever to arrive at this expanded consciousness, we will have to surrender our ego desires to the wisdom of the Self. Masculine and Feminine will have to learn to cherish each other.
> —*Marion Woodman*

Part III

THE GODDESS RULES

SIX PRACTICES FOR BECOMING YOUR MOST AMAZING SELF

The Goddess does not rule the world;
She is the world.
—*Starhawk*

The Goddess is not just the female version of God.
She represents a different concept.
—*Merlin Stone*

This is what the goddess really is . . .
a network of connective intelligence that
is operating on this planet.
—*Terence McKenna*

FROM MY HEART TO YOURS

When the Goddess rules, humankind lives in partnership with all life.
When the Goddess rules, we live from a place of stillness and spirit of embrace.
When the Goddess rules, we fiercely protect innocence and truth.
When the Goddess rules, we know we are one in this
great whirling mystery called life.
Suzin Green, *The Goddess Rules Blog*

Back in 2009, when print media was going down and digital was on the rise, I wanted an online space where people could read magazine articles I'd written on the Goddess. So I started a blog called *The Goddess Rules*. Once I uploaded those articles, I moved on to other projects. That quirky double entendre of a name however, stayed with me.

Fast forward fifteen years later.

I always assumed the final part of this book would be a self-guided course, offering a collection of inner work exercises, guided meditations, and journal-writing prompts. When I got here however, I just wasn't feeling it. For the next several months I sat at my laptop day after day, facing that blank page, writing and writing. But there was no energy in any of it, no juice.

Then one evening around sunset I was out walking and the Goddess Rules—not "rules" as in one who rules over others, but "rules" as in rules of the game—channeled through me. They came fast and furious in what seemed a nanosecond. I was so concerned I might forget them, I repeated them over and over as I made my way home. At that point in the process they struck me as a fun little extra to include in a sidebar. As I lived with them, however, fleshing them into chapters and marveling at their wisdom, I began to understand that they are much more than a fun little extra. The Goddess Rules are a powerful mind/body medicine that zooms in on the essential themes of this book. In fact, they carry its living essence. These six practices are the integration of being and doing this book is ultimately about. Living into them will guide you toward embodying whatever insight you've found in its pages. A thousand times more interesting than any workbook I might have created, the Goddess Rules are also a parting gift that the writing of this book gave to me, and now I get to give that gift to you.

There is some serious wonder here.

I've been fascinated by the mystery of creative process for much of my adult life. I've studied it, taught it, been informed by it, lived inside of it. And still, after all these years, it always takes me by surprise.

And so, I offer you the Goddess Rules. If the goddess remedy is a medicinal, then they are its active ingredient. While living in their wisdom is the work of a lifetime, as the old saying goes, "The journey of a thousand miles begins with the first step." And so, from my heart to yours, let's start walking. . .

THE GODDESS RULES

Building the Container
#1: **Zip It**

Opening into Being
#2: **Feel Your Feelings**

The Kālī Work
#3: **Get Over Yourself**

The Lakṣmī Work
#4: **Count Your Blessings and Clean Your House**

The Saraswatī Work
#5: **Stop Talking and Start Listening**

The Kuan Yin Work
#6: **It's Not About You, It's About the World**

Chapter 14

Building the Container #1: ZIP IT

The container is an essential piece of our doing function. It's the boundary of self, the "I" of "I am." If you want to cultivate a healthy container, a container that fosters the integration we've been talking about throughout this book, a container that holds you serene and powerful as you move through each day, here's the secret: Zip it.

Zip up the need to be right.

Nothing turns our container into a colander like this particular category of verbal aggression. Leak. Leak. Leak. The need to be right tricks us into believing we're the smartest person in the room. Odds are, we're not. The smartest person in the room has no need to show their smarts.

There's an old saying that goes: Most people would rather be right than happy. Choose happy. It's more fun and keeps your container doing what it's meant to do: contain.

The need to be right is actually a defense against the fear of not knowing, the fear of not being seen, the fear of annihilation. When we go down this particular rabbit hole, we end up more lost than found.

Be curious. It's way more interesting. It's also a much more powerful stance. When you need to be right, people perceive you as boorish and keep their distance. Whereas people who are curious draw others to them. People who are curious tend to light up the room. Because their container is not leaking, all their light shines through.

Zip up displacing and discharging your anxiety and anger onto other people.

The world is not your toxic waste dump. Why make a mess when you can live clean and lovely?

Do the inner work that enables you to process raw uncomfortable emotions. Don't let your patriarchal masculine run with them and worse, weaponize them against you and the people you like and love, and for that matter, the people you don't like and love. Contain, contain, contain. This is the secret of inner transformation. This is how anxiety and anger morph into clarity, determination, and will. Sit with the discomfort of raw emotion. Feel it. Don't leak it. Hold it. Don't leak it. You can do this. It just takes practice. You want to be seen. You want to be heard. You want to be taken seriously. Don't leak it. Zip it.

Zip up giving advice, especially of the unsolicited type.

Truth is, no one is all that interested. Mostly what happens when we offer unsolicited advice is that people shut down. This is their defense against our implication that they're doing something wrong. The next time you find yourself offering advice and suggestions, have a look at where the impulse is coming from inside of you and zip it.

If someone wants your opinion or advice, they'll ask for it. Even then, less is more. We all need to find our own way. It's how we humans work. We tend to learn from making mistakes, falling down, standing back up, and moving on. When we offer unsolicited advice, suggestions, and/or fixes, we take this away from the people we're trying to help. The way we help other people is by listening to them, seeing them, trusting in them, and believing in them. What we all need is to be seen and embraced. What we all don't need are people who think they know better than we do.

This doesn't mean we should never offer counsel and guidance to our children, to people around us who are floundering, or to those who actually ask for our help. It simply means that it's generally a good idea to move toward listening and away from fixing. Every now and then, offering solutions or advice is just the medicine a person needs. More often, however, when we offer solutions and advice, we stand in the way of a person finding their way.

And did I say that offering unsolicited advice and suggestions is another way we poke holes in our container? It is. Big gaping holes. Zip it.

Zip up the judgy voice of your mean-girl self.

She may be a girl, but trust me, she's a piece of the inner patriarch. I get it, we all love a good gossip fest. But really, being critical of others to make ourselves feel better makes our container smaller. And a smaller container squeezes and misshapes its contents. And in this case, those contents happen to be us.

When we're critical of others in that mean-girl kind of way, what we're actually doing is projecting our worst fears about ourselves onto them. This is important, so I'll say it again: When we're critical of others in that mean-girl kind of way, what we're actually doing is projecting our worst fears about ourselves onto them. Oops. Zip it.

Needless to say, this is one of the patriarchal masculine's favorite tricks. Why own up to stuff we don't much like about ourselves so we can initiate the necessary changes? Oh no. The patriarchal masculine prefers we avoid the inward gaze. This is why it loves projection. When we project our own whatever onto whatever poor sod is in our view, we cut ourselves off from the depth and power of our own, well, our own depth and power. Not good.

You want to weaken and contract your container, give in to the judgy voice of your mean-girl self. You want to be a luminous being, then, as the old saying goes, never judge another until you've walked a mile in their shoes. In other words, when the mean-girl impulse rises up inside you, take a look at where it's coming from and zip it.

And just to clarify . . .

There's a big difference between judgy mean-girl talk and discernment. Judgy mean-girl talk is driven by the patriarchal masculine. It's mean-spirited nastiness masquerading as harmless gossip, put-downs, and jokes at another's expense.

Discernment, on the other hand, is integration at its finest. It's the faculty of mind that helps us navigate our way through the terrain of daily life. Discernment is wisdom and clarity channeling through a clean and shining container. When we discern a person or situation is not working for us, gossiping about them won't help. What we need to do is strategize a safe and seamless exit.

Zip up oversharing and/or giving too much information.

As a general rule, keep it short and simple. In conversation, texting, email, in any way you communicate with words, less is more. And please, no defending, no explaining, and do keep the "I'm sorrys" to a minimum. This category of leaking is very weakening of the container. So take your foot out of your mouth and zip it.

Zip up worrying about what other people think of you.

This one's a big source of container leakage. I would go so far as to say it leans toward container siphoning. Not to mention it's a waste of energy and time. So the next time you find yourself worrying about what someone thinks about you, pause for a moment and ask yourself this question: "Don't they have anything better to do with their time?" And then zip it.

There's also the deeper piece about how worrying what others think of us is actually a projection of our own self-doubt, self-judgment, self-loathing, etc. The patriarchal masculine loves this because when we project this stuff out, we cut ourselves off from the possibility of sorting ourselves out. This is definitely in the "not good" category. So, yes, you know what to do: Zip it.

Zip up putting everyone else's needs ahead of your own.

You know how before an airplane takes off, they say that if the oxygen masks drop down, put your own on before you help those around you? This always struck me as counterintuitive bordering on selfish. Until I realized that if I'm passed out from oxygen deprivation, I can't help anyone else. Yup. Got it.

We can certainly fault the airline industry for prioritizing corporate profit over passenger comfort, not to mention carbon footprint and related environmental degradation. On the oxygen mask point, however, the airlines get it 100 percent right. On the airplane and in life, when the oxygen mask drops down, put your own on first. In other words, when you find yourself putting everyone else's needs ahead of your own, take a look at what's driving this compulsion and zip it.

This doesn't mean we should lean into narcissistic self-absorption, greed, and selfishness. Of course not. We need to live carefully. We need to live thoughtfully. We need to live with a sense of honor and respect, to cultivate good old-fashioned manners. This makes us all-around better people. Because we're contained. So we're all here. Here. Not over there. Here. Which means our action, our doing function, is a clear, clean channel for the majesty and beauty, the clarity and power, the amazing amazingness that we actually are. And the amazing amazingness that we actually are is very precious cargo. So we don't want to leak it. Did we say zip it? Yes, zip it.

Zip up the voice of the patriarchal masculine.

The voice of the patriarchal masculine hijacks us into all the aforementioned habits of mind. This is an inner voice that wants us believing its voice belongs to us. It does not. Its voice belongs to the inner patriarch. Its voice fosters the lie that there is something wrong with us. There is nothing wrong with us. There may be patterns and behaviors we want to change. There may be deeper psycho-emotional issues we want to address. But none of this means there is anything wrong with us. All this means is that we need to give ourselves loving and careful attention. All this means is that we need to learn how to truly listen to ourselves. All this means is that we've been seduced into belief systems and narratives that are wrong.

So when that knurly, tricky, deceitful, deceptive, seductive, cajoling, belittling, aggrandizing, annoying, demeaning, distracting, denying, avoiding, addicting, drama-creating, and sweet-talking impostor of your true voice attempts to take you over, take a long, deep breath, lob a few repetitions of *om srī kālī mā* in its direction, and zip it.

Building Blocks of the Container

- Attention
- Discipline
- Listening
- Taking care
- Determination
- The patience to build good habits
- Attention to detail
- Knowing ourselves
- Fearlessness to speak truth to ourselves
- Moving slowly and carefully

Signs of Container Leakage and Malfunction

- Oversharing
- Needing to be the center of attention
- Talking over others
- Talking to fill the space
- Not listening to what other people are saying
- Self-referencing rather than openhearted listening
- Telling the same stories over and over
- Offering unsolicited advice
- Finishing other people's sentences

- Second-guessing every decision
- Making a mess of everything (or much of what) we set out to do
- Putting everyone else's needs ahead of our own, as in saying "yes" when we want to say "no"
- On the other hand, allowing ourselves to be ruled by self-absorption, cruelty, deception, and greed
- Or allowing ourselves to be ruled by worry, anxiety, and self-doubt
- Or unable to do what we want to be doing
- Or acting in ways that make us (and others) suffer

Chapter 15

Opening into Being
#2: FEEL YOUR FEELINGS

Most of us conflate feeling with thought, a patriarchal mind trick that lulls us into dissociating from our feelings before we've had a chance to, well, feel them. Since our feelings are the "am" of "I am," dissociating from them is a losing strategy for living wise, living empowered, living free—because feeling our feelings is the only way we come to know ourselves. Feeling our feelings—even the so-called negative ones—keeps our container in excellent working order. In fact, feeling our feelings strengthens the entire body/mind system. Because without the "am" of our feelings, we're an empty shell. Feeling our feelings is the best reality check there is.

If we want to live skillfully, if we want to live authentically, if we want to live with heart, we need to feel our feelings. Feel them. Not dissociate from them. Listen to them. Not deny them. Embrace them. Not project them. Respect them. Not push them away.

These forms of avoidance are beloved ploys of the inner patriarch. It works overtime to corrupt our container, turning what should be a clutter-free, feeling-friendly environment, an environment where feelings move gracefully from ground, to belly, to heart, to mind, into a murky mess. A mess that zigzags and dead-ends our feelings, squishing them into clogged pockets of projection, dissociation, and those repetitive internal dialogues that keep us down.

Feel your feelings. Don't hand them over to the inner patriarch.

And while we're talking about feelings, let's also talk about their relationship with power. Not the patriarchal greed for domination and control kind of power. The power that is fed by kindness, curiosity, and compassion. The power that we recognize in people who are 100 percent comfortable in their own skin. The power that we feel in beauty, simplicity, and truth. The power that we know as stillness, wisdom, and love. This is the power of our own presence, the power inherent in the inner ground. Our feelings are the portal into our ground. When we cut ourselves off from our feelings, we shut the door on our power.

Thought that's freed itself from patriarchal conditioning understands its relationship to feeling. Although the two are intimately connected, thought is not feeling and feeling is not thought. Much as patriarchy would have us believe otherwise, thought can only discern right action when it takes its cues from feeling. The idea that feeling is inferior to thought is one of patriarchy's big lies. The truth is, thought that is wise, clarifying, and interesting, evocative, inspired, and intelligent, joyous, gentle, and powerful, luminous, moving, and brilliant, is absolutely dependent on feeling.

"I feel like . . ." is not a feeling.

Pay attention and you'll notice how often you say or hear others say, "I feel like . . ." Okay, take this in: "I feel like . . ." is not a feeling. It's a thought pretending to be a feeling. And the feeling is always more interesting than the point this languaging will never make. "I feel like . . ." is one of the patriarch's trickiest tricks. Simply placing that innocuous word "like" after "I feel" robs what we're actually feeling of its clarity and power.

This may strike you as a ridiculous point to quibble over. It's not. It's baseline important for knowing ourselves.

You say, "I feel like this is something I shouldn't be doing." No, you *think* this is something you shouldn't be doing. What you're feeling is discomfort. Big difference. Own the discomfort—as in "I'm feeling really uncomfortable right now"—and you might just pull yourself back from whatever it is that you'd rather not be doing. Keep it at the "I feel like . . ." level and the odds are you'll keep doing it.

Owning our feelings protects us. Denying our feelings, not so much.

You say, "I feel like getting out of the house." Again, not a feeling. What are you actually feeling, and will getting out of the house give you what you actually need? Not if there's stuff in the house that needs your immediate attention. Better to start with, "What am I feeling that's making me want to get out of the house? Oh, I'm feeling anxious. Why? Because I have a long list of household tasks I've been avoiding, and just thinking about the pileup makes me feel anxious and want to flee. Hmmm. Maybe what I need to do is stay home and tackle the to-do list. Ah. I feel better already."

Here's one more.

"I feel like he didn't really mean that." What are we actually feeling when we say, "I feel like he didn't really mean that"? Confusion maybe, as in, What did he actually mean? Leery maybe, as in, I hope that's not what he meant. Appalled perhaps, as in, he better not have meant that.

When very interesting feelings like "confusion," "leery," or "appalled" get morphed into bland ideas like "I feel like he didn't really mean that," we drain the life out of our experience, leaving ourselves with no clear way to discern our next move. If we feel confusion, we need to ask for clarification, not make some vague value judgment about what someone said. If we feel leery, we had better do more than ask for clarification. We had better be sure this is someone we can actually trust. And if we're feeling appalled, we might want to exit immediately.

And for the record, in cases like this, when we say, "I feel like he, she, or they blah blah blah," rather than "I'm feeling blah blah blah," we're making it about "them" rather than about us. And when we make it about them rather than about us, we cancel ourselves out of the equation. This is patriarchal self-gaslighting par excellence. Do yourself a favor, lose the "like" after "I feel."

What are you feeling right now? Can you name it? Or do you draw a blank? And is the feeling you think you're feeling a feeling? Or is it a thought masquerading as a feeling? Odds are, it's a thought.

Here's a short list of feelings you may be experiencing as you sit here reading or listening to this book:

- Bored
- Confused
- Distracted
- Empowered
- Encouraged
- Engaged
- Inspired
- Overwhelmed
- Restless

Try it. Make a list of feelings you're having right now. Did the words flow or did you draw a blank? Are the words you wrote feelings? Or do they fall into the thought category of commentary, analysis, observation, or critique? We want to train ourselves to discern the difference, so the patriarch can never trick us into dissociating from our feelings.

Trust your feelings. Unlike the mind, they never lie.

A few weeks after I met the man I would later marry, I went to visit him in Boston, where he lived. He took me to his favorite beach. It was a wild and beautiful place. Being there, however, I felt the tiniest sense of foreboding. Yet I was so blissed out, so lost in the endorphin-driven rapture of new love, I ignored this feeling.

At one point I ran down to the water's edge, kneeling in the sand and running my hands through the surf. I assumed he was right behind me. When I turned around, however, he hadn't moved. Coming back to where he was standing, I felt a fleeting sense of shock and dread all through me. This went so against my "and they lived happily ever after" narrative that I simply could not, would not, absolutely refused to admit what I was actually experiencing in that discomfiting moment.

I never forgot it, though. So many times during our thirty-year marriage, I remembered that glimpse of the chasm between us. I will not say our time together was all bad. There were good years. There were fine times. Perhaps there were lessons I could only learn through this long, difficult relationship. However, had I heeded that early alarm bell, I doubt I would have hung in there for thirty years trying to bridge an impossible gap.

There is no such thing as a bad or negative feeling.

Listening to our feelings is not always what we're in the mood for. Especially when we don't want to hear what they're saying. How many times have you heard (or said to yourself) things like, "You're too emotional, too sensitive, too angry," or "You have no right to feel that way," or "You're overreacting, being irrational, behaving like a child."

Do not, I repeat, do not listen to this messaging. It is all wrong. It's the voice of the wounding masculine. We have to stay with our feelings to discern what they're saying. This doesn't mean we should act on them immediately. As a general rule, we should not.

And it certainly doesn't mean we should leak, act out, or wallow in them. It simply means that it's always a good idea to lean in and listen.

When I was twenty years old, soon after I married my first husband, I developed eczema on the fourth finger of my left hand, right under my wedding band. Over the next couple of years, the eczema spread over both hands. A clear statement if ever there was one. I tried many remedies—cortisone cream; zinc tablets; eliminating wheat, dairy, and citrus from my diet; even washing my hands with bleach. Some worked a little; others worked not at all. The bleach was a disaster. The day I got divorced, the eczema disappeared.

Feelings we do not allow ourselves to acknowledge have a way of growing into the inner obstructions that cause or at least contribute to physical, emotional, and psychological problems as well as to creative and spiritual blocks. Listen to your feelings. Especially the ones you want to avoid. Like I said earlier: Unlike the mind, they never lie.

Sometimes a situation is untenable, yet for a host of reasons, we're unable to move on. In these situations, acknowledging the truth of our feelings, no matter how uncomfortable they may be, allows us to see a situation for what it is. This will make a difference in our survival.

Needless to say, I don't wish bullying and abuse on anyone. However, if for whatever reason we find ourselves in a toxic situation with no seeming way out, the clarity of awareness we glean through listening to our feelings will foster the inner strength we need to find our way. In situations like these, every feeling we pay serious attention to is another step toward the empowering force of the "enough" moment.

Bottom line 1: Listening to our feelings is the only way we can truly know ourselves.

Bottom line 2: The inner patriarch is dead set against us doing this.

Bottom line 3: Never allow the inner patriarch to own you.

Bottom line 4: Own your feelings and you own yourself.

Snip, snip, snip.

One of my favorite aspects of the Kālī archetype is called Tārā Mahāvidyā. Along with Kālī's always present sword, she often carries a pair of scissors. You have to love that image: Goddess with Scissors.

All these cutting implements serve one function: They cut the ties that bind us to everything and anyone that dares to cause us harm. Listening to, naming, and honoring our feelings is the way we wield those scissors and swords inside ourselves. And those scissors and swords are some of the best tools for shaping our most authentic self and for maintaining proper boundaries around that self.

When we trace the harm-causers down to their toxic root, we always find the evil puppet master—let's call it by its true name, the wounding/wounded patriarchal masculine—pulling the strings. So feel your feelings, pull out those scissors, and snip, snip, snip.

Take a moment to think about your own personal harm-causers. If you're so inclined, you might make a list of your top three.

Here's a list to get you started. Snip, snip, snip . . .

- Stultifying habits
- Deadening addictions
- Toxic relationships
- Rigid belief systems
- Too much doing
- Not enough being
- Compulsions
- Denial
- Avoidance
- Projection
- Fear of failure
- Fear of success
- Forgetting who and what you truly are

Chapter 16

The Kālī Work

#3: GET OVER YOURSELF

It is always a danger
To aspirants
On the
Path
When they begin
To believe and
Act
As if the ten thousand idiots
Who so long ruled
And lived
Inside
Have all packed their bags
And skipped town . . .
—*Hafiz/Ladinsky*

Let's pause for a moment to reflect on a world where everyone whose actions cause harm would just get over themselves. You know, work through their psycho-emotional wounding, feel what they're actually feeling, zip up their projections, assumptions, and the need to be right, and, well, just get over themselves.

Think of the warrior goddess in the great battle between the gods and demons. She demolishes the entire demon army without breaking a sweat, pausing for that poignant moment at the end to nurse the crying infant, and then, voilà, she is gone. No fuss, no muss, no transactional quid pro quo or accolades required.

om srī kālī mā

This is how we want to live. It really is so much simpler. Yogis refer to the spaciousness of mind embodied in the archetype we personify as the goddess Kālī as *sthita prajna*, steady wisdom. Steady wisdom is the epitome of getting over ourselves, the antithesis of the drama queen mode so many of us live in. There's a tremendous sense of freedom here, a profound embrace of the way things actually are. There is no praise, no blame. There is simply what is. Which begs the question: Why live in drama when we can live in what is?

But drama is the way of the patriarch. It prefers we live in story, wrestling with ourselves in the least productive ways. You know, living unzipped and unfeeling (except of course for feeling sorry for ourselves), judging everything and everyone (most of all, secretly, ourselves), worrying about whoever and whatever, and living overall with a very thin skin that leaves us reactive and often ridiculous.

I'm sorry to tell you this, but you and I and everyone else are little more than specks in the cosmic sea. We really don't matter. No matter what we've achieved. No matter what we may be achieving. The only thing that matters is how well we loved, how thoughtfully we listened, how much we gave back, how often we allowed our hearts to open. Everything else is dust.

So really, when the inner patriarch tricks you into being way too precious about this or that, about me or mine, about my way or the highway, take a few deep breaths, shoot a few more repetitions of *om srī kālī mā* in its direction, and just get over yourself.

om srī kālī mā

> Because this business of becoming conscious . . . is
> ultimately about asking yourself,
> How alive am I willing to be?
> —*Anne Lamott*

Chapter 17

The Lakṣmī Work

#4: COUNT YOUR BLESSINGS AND CLEAN YOUR HOUSE

Hello, sun in my face.
Hello, you who make the morning
and spread it over the fields
and into the faces of the tulips
and the nodding morning glories,
and into the windows of, even, the
miserable and the crotchety . . .
—Mary Oliver

Let's pause for a moment to take a page from the sun's playbook. In the way it offers its light, as the poet says, to "even, the miserable and the crotchety . . ." Which doesn't mean we have to like everyone. Or agree with them. Or allow them to run roughshod over anyone or anything in their way. It simply means we keep shining. It simply means we allow nothing to obliterate our light.

So, count your blessings and clean your house.

And by "house," we're not just talking about the roof-over-our-head type. We're talking about the house of the body, house of the mind, house of the heart, house of the family, house of the community, and house of this planet we all call home. So many rooms in these seven houses and all requiring our careful attention.

Sure, we have plenty to do. Sure, it can be really demanding. Sure, it often requires we do what we're not in the mood to do. Although just because we're not in the mood doesn't mean it doesn't need to be done. And since it's generally the inner patriarch that drives the mood, the jury's out on the credibility of said mood. In other words, when you find you're not in the mood to do what needs to be done, it's time to get over yourself. I mean, really, just like the sun, this business of living is never done. Why foster poor me wailings when you can just count your blessings and get on with it?

You're still here. You're breathing. If you're reading this book, the odds are you have a roof over your head, clothes on your back, food in the refrigerator, a bed to sleep on, a source of income, and the wide-open possibility of this present moment. So count your blessings. And get back to cleaning. In fact, keep counting those blessings while you clean. You'll do a much better job.

And live with your eyes wide open as you count your blessings and clean your house.

This is where Lakṣmī—whose eyes, you may remember from Chapter 10, remain always open—comes into the mix. Lakṣmī, you may also remember, has a very impressive resume. As in being a personification of qualities like magnificence and grace; as in being a seed within us, which when properly tended, grows us into our most beautiful self. Beauty that is way more than skin deep. Beauty that is synonymous with truth.

If the idea of leaning into fabulous appeals to you, this is an energy field you want to cultivate. Which, for starters, requires paying careful attention to every aspect of our lives, also known as living with eyes wide open. So let's count our blessings, keep cleaning those houses (all seven of them), and leave every room more shining and beautiful than we found it.

Don't rush through the cleaning.

Counting your blessings while you clean will help with this one. Move slowly. Move thoughtfully. Move with graceful alignment of body, heart, and mind. Push back against distraction. Push back against dissociation and spacing out. Push back against the endless prattle of the mind. Pay attention. Be where you are. Smile. And renounce rushing. Rushing fuels anxiety and leaves a mess in its wake. Plus, there is nowhere to go that rushing will get you to faster. Lakṣmī never rushes and always arrives on time.

And while counting your blessings, be sure to include the mud.

Always remember that beneath that lovely exterior, Lakṣmī, an embodiment of the most beautiful, vital, vibrant, ambrosial, sublime, is rooted in the mud. Leaning into fabulous requires we always keep at least one foot in the mud. Leaning into fabulous requires that we always remember we're part mud. The mud is the fertile darkness, the source of all life. We're all one in the mud. So while you're counting and cleaning, help someone else count and clean too. Share your bounty and offer it with unconditional love.

Become the blessing.

It's fine to count your blessings to make yourself feel better. Just don't stop there. Count your blessings to become the blessing. To embody the blessing. Embodying the blessing makes everyone and everything around us feel better. Because it's no longer about us. It's about we.

Embodying the blessing also pushes back against the patriarch's driving narrative: that we're not enough, that we don't have enough, that there's something wrong with us, and that the only thing that will fix us is more more more and better better better.

Now let me be clear here. More and better are not the problem. It's the striving after more and better that creates the problem. It's the idea that there's something out there that will make us (finally) complete that's the problem. Striving and its partner attachment are the problem.

The irony is there really is no problem. Lakṣmī is more and better. Lakṣmī is the blessing. It's right here inside us. We don't have to strive after it. We just have to embody it. So become the blessing and the clean house. It's never about striving. It's only about becoming.

Living 100 percent comfortable in our own skin.

Lakṣmī's a great model for this one. Because Lakṣmī is 100 percent comfortable in its energetic skin. Easier said than done, although her creation myth spells it out quite clearly. If you don't remember that story, you'll find it back in Chapter 10.

Here's the CliffsNotes version: Lakṣmī becomes possible through an alliance between the gods (code for what we like about ourselves) and the demons (code for what we don't), who must join together to churn the ocean of milk (code for cleaning all seven houses) in order to discover the precious dew of life (code for Lakṣmī), who will also require we drink the poison (code for patriarchal masculine) before she deigns to enter into our mind/body mix.

Got it . . .

I know, it's a lot to process. Just keep cleaning and counting, cleaning and counting, cleaning and counting. That's the path. You're on your way.

And always remember Dhūmāvatī.

In the Lakṣmī chapter in Part II, I wrote that in order to fully embody Lakṣmī, we have to embrace her nonidentical twin sisters, Alakṣmī and Dhūmāvatī, and said we'd come back to Dhūmāvatī in Part III.

First, however, a recap of Alakṣmī. In Sanskrit, when an "a" is placed before a noun, it denotes what we think of as the opposite or negation of that which the noun is naming. So if Lakṣmī is the promise of youth, Alakṣmī is the dissolution that comes with old age. If Lakṣmī is the fullness of life, Alakṣmī is emptiness and death. In this binary framing, we're trained to shun these negatives. The problem is, the negative is the other half. The problem is, we don't have one without the other. When we don't want to see her as she actually is, Alakṣmī fills us with revulsion. When we open our eyes, we realize there is nothing to shun here and everything to embrace.

> This place where you are right now
> God circled on a map for you.
> Wherever your eyes and arms and heart can move
> Against the earth and sky,
> The Beloved has bowed there—
> Our Beloved has bowed there knowing
> You were coming.
> —*Hafiz/Ladinsky*

Dhūmāvatī is the haute couture version of Alakṣmī. Her name translates as "the smoky one." Let's sit with that for a moment. If you take the mud of the fertile darkness, extract its most concentrated essence, distill that essence to its molecular structure, find the gravitational center of that structure, light its center on fire, and let the invisible smoke spread into infinity, you begin to touch into the energetic field that is Dhūmāvatī.

I know, it's a lot to comprehend.

Bottom line: Dhūmāvatī is the essence of the essence of the essence of all the stuff of life we're taught to dread: darkness, disease, decay, decrepitude, dissolution, and dying. Which makes her anathema to the patriarchal mind. Because more than anything else, the mind formed in patriarchy fears its own death. Every patriarchal structure, from the societal level of patriarchy to the individual level of inner patriarch, is driven by the need to deny death. Death of the body, death of the mind, death of a loved one, death of identity, death of the empire, death of whatever we cling to. The problem with this denial of death, however, is that it tends to be, well, a dead end. Hard as we may try, the truth is, we can't get away from it.

Every wisdom tradition I've encountered tells us that if we want to become fully human, we have got to make friends with death. That death is the great teacher of life. Death reminds us that every moment is a gift. That everyone and everything is part of that gift. And that we're all connected in the beautiful mud.

Like yesterday, when I went for an afternoon walk. There were a lot of people out, many of them tourists, who were stopping on the sidewalk to take group shots and selfies. This always triggers my inner mean-girl's rant about their insensitivity to those of us who need to keep moving. I'd been working on this chapter for the last few days, however, and was deep in Dhūmāvatī's smoky weeds. In that spaciousness, I just couldn't summon the usual annoyance. The only thing I felt was love.

Yes.

Love.

So keep counting those blessings and cleaning those houses and always remember that Dhūmāvatī is right here, blessing and cleaning and walking beside us every step of the way.

om srī lakṣmī mā
om srī alakṣmī mā
om srī dhūmāvatī mā

Friend, hope for the Guest while you are alive. Jump
into experience while you are alive!
Think . . . and think . . . while you are alive
What you call "salvation" belongs to the time
before death.

If you don't break your ropes while you're alive, do
you think ghosts will do it after?

The idea that the soul will join with the ecstatic
just because the body is rotten—
that is all fantasy.
What is found now is found then.
If you find nothing now,
you will simply end up with an apartment in the
City of Death.
If you make love with the divine now, in the next
life you will have the face of satisfied desire.

So plunge into the truth, find out who the Teacher
is, believe in the Great Sound!

Kabir says this: When the Guest is being searched
for, it is the intensity of the longing for the Guest
that does all the work.
Look at me, and you will see a slave of that intensity.
—Kabir/Bly

Chapter 18

The Saraswatī Work
#5: STOP TALKING AND START LISTENING

Take your busy heart to the art museum and the chamber of commerce
but take it also to the forest.
The song you heard singing in the leaf when you were a child
is singing still.
—Mary Oliver

Listening is a precious gift.

Most of us take this business of listening for granted. But listening, true listening, is what wakes us up to the world. Along the way it's how we learn to hear the wisdom of our bodies. It's how we let another know we see them and they matter. It's how we discern that which is true from that which pretends to be.

I had a client who came to see me every week. We'd talk the first half of his session and do Eyes-Closed Work the second. One morning we were so engrossed in conversation, I didn't realize we'd talked through his entire time. When I apologized for robbing him of Eyes-Closed time, he said, "What are you talking about? Do you have any idea how it feels to talk with someone who's actually listening?"

Right. Point taken.

We tend to equate listening with hearing. They're related for sure. But hearing is more passive. Hearing happens whether or not we're actually listening. Listening is a choice. Listening requires we pay attention. Listening requires we open ourselves to receive. And the quality of our openness is the difference between someone who actually hears and someone who's just passing the time.

I studied with a composer who was one of the greatest listeners I've ever known. He heard everything. The words spoken and the life behind the words. The music made and the silence that held it. The first time I sang for him, he smiled and said, "Ah, you sing the *canto jondo*." I'd never heard that term and asked him what it was. "The deep song," he said, "you sing the deep song."

> [The Deep Song] . . . is deep, truly deep, more so than any well, more so than all the seas that bathe the world, deeper than the present spirit that creates it or the voice that sings it, because it is well-nigh infinite.
>
> —*Federico Garcia Lorca*

When we pay attention, we begin to discern the deep song singing inside and all around us. We may not hear it with our physical ears. We may have to listen through our belly or our heart. But singing, always, it is here. We can even learn to discern it in the cacophony of daily life, not to mention cacophony of our minds. So let's have a listening party. Turn off your phone, close your eyes, and listen . . .

Listening makes miracles happen.

Listening is a judgment-free zone. It's also a fluid one. Any agenda, any sticky stuff, any hardening, clogs the listening space. Listening, true listening, requires us to step out of opinion and beliefs, out of the need to look good or be right, out of distraction, frustration, annoyance, and self-absorption. True listening, whether we're listening to ourself, listening to another, or listening to the world, requires us to be present and receiving. When it comes to listening, not to mention living, flexible curiosity and the need to *not* be right is a powerful stance.

Try this: The next time you're feeling out of sorts, make an effort to listen to someone. Anyone. Doesn't have to be a person you know. Whoever it is, wherever they are, just listen, engaging with your full attention. You'll be amazed at how much better you feel. And you'll make their day too.

Several years ago, my health insurance company dropped our neighborhood pharmacy from their approved vendors list. This meant that if I didn't switch to a retail chain, the cost of my prescription drugs would skyrocket. I was opposed to this on so many levels, I decided to push back. After several futile conversations with service reps, I filed a formal appeal. The response to that was a form letter denial. I found that letter so insulting, I decided to write to the vice president whose signature was on it, cc'ing the CEO and president of the board. A few weeks later, much to my amazement, I received an apologetic call from the vice president, telling me she was fast-tracking my appeal, and assuring me my pharmacy would be reinstated in the new year.

I was so moved by her call, I bought an exquisite card and handwrote a note expressing my profound gratitude and adding my hope that receiving a card like this in the midst of her workday would be a wonderful surprise. A few days later she called again. The delight in her voice was palpable. Just hearing it made me feel so happy. And there we were, two strangers, who'd managed through our listening—she to my plea, me to her humanity—to make a connection I suspect neither of us will ever forget. A small miracle.

I'm not so naive to believe that in the battle against privatized healthcare this is more than a miniscule drop in the bucket. She heard me and reinstated my pharmacy. I heard her and sent a beautiful card. Who but us, and honestly, probably mostly me, actually cares? But here's the thing. Every time we stop to listen—to ourself, to another, to everything around us—we add a small miracle to the miracle pool of the world. That's a very luminous pool. And one of these days, the miracle pool will finally tip over, flooding the world with its light. Until that day, I figure the least we can do is keep listening, remembering that every act of listening adds another miracle to the pool.

Take the listening quiz.

1. How well do you listen?
On a scale of 1–10 with 1 being completely checked out and 10 being completely engaged, where do you land?

2. Do you love hearing yourself talk:
    a) Most of the time
    b) Some of the time
    c) Rarely
    d) Never

3. Do you love listening to others:
    a) Most of the time
    b) Some of the time
    c) Rarely
    d) Never

4. In conversation with others, check all that apply to you:
    a) I want to leave the room.
    b) I can't wait for them to finish talking so I can share my related experience.
    c) I tend to finish their sentences before they're done speaking.
    d) I lecture and pontificate.
    e) I like to pacify, offer solutions, and give advice.
    f) I tend to disagree and negate what others are saying.
    g) I listen with curiosity.
    h) I work hard to listen so I can truly hear what they're saying, even when I disagree.

The singing leaf might also be listening.

One of the great things about listening is that it's not a solitary act. It's an act of communion. And who's to say that only we of the animal realm can listen? Who's to say that singing leaf is not listening too? And for that matter, who's to say that everything, sentient, nonsentient, and everything in between is not also listening? Which is why we want to live with care and purpose, to tread softly, speak thoughtfully, and be really mindful of the echoes that billow in our wake. We never know who or what is listening.

This is where the dharma of speech, which you hopefully remember from the Saraswatī chapter in Part II, comes in very handy: *Speak only that which is kind, true, necessary, and at the appropriate time.*

Yes.

One of the teachings that drew me to the yogic path was the Tantric notion that everything, whether animal, vegetable, or mineral, is created from pulsating, shimmering consciousness. In other words, at the deepest level we're all made of the same shimmering stuff. I would later find this idea in other wisdom traditions and then, much later, in theoretical physicist Brian Greene's work. It really does give one pause. It's not just that we're all one, as in "We Are the World" all one. It's way deeper than that. We really are all one.

> When you recognize that we emerged from particles . . . from just after the Big Bang, and those particles, through the force of gravity, clustered together into certain pockets of order called stars and certain other pockets of order called planets, and on some of those planets, those particles . . . yielded ever more refined particles, and some collection of those particles began to think and breathe and live and wonder

> about reality, you recognize that we all came from the same place. We're literally all the same. . . . You recognize that the adage that we are all together, it's not just a Hallmark card. We are literally all part of the very same physical process.
> — *Brian Greene*

Whether we can actually hear the song of the leaf is irrelevant. Our job is to keep listening. Listening with our whole body. Listening with our belly, ears, heart, and mind. Listening to the multitude of creation. Listening to the silence. Slowing down so we can actually hear. When I listen to you, even if I disagree with every word you're saying, through that listening, doors open and communion might just happen. If not today, maybe tomorrow. Listening is the great reminder that we really are all one. So let's renew our membership in the Deep Song of the World Chorus. We're all singing together anyway. Why settle for noise when we can make beautiful music?

om srī saraswatī mā

Chapter 19

The Kuan Yin Work

#6: IT'S NOT ABOUT YOU, IT'S ABOUT THE WORLD

Every day I am astonished by
how little I know, and discouraged, obedient as I am to the demand to
know more—always more.
But then there is the slow seep
of light from the day,
and I look to the west where
the hills are darkening,
setting their shoulders to the night,
and the sky peppered with pillows
of mist, their bellies burnt
by the furnace of the sun.
And it is then that I notice
the invitation didn't say, Come
armed with knowledge and a loud voice.
It only said, Come.
—Andrew Colliver

It's not about you, it's about the world.

We can point out the obvious. Look up from your phone. Smile at people you pass on the street, maybe even say "hello." Consider the journey that everything you consume has taken. For that matter, take a page from the Iroquois Nation and consider the impact of everything you do—not just everything you consume, everything you do—on the next seven generations. Be respectful of others (even when you disagree). Be kind (even when you're angry). Be curious (even when you're afraid). Be courteous (even when you're triggered). Be thoughtful (even when you tend toward selfish). Be generous (even when you tend toward stingy). These all go without saying.

But let's take it deeper . . .

This Goddess Rule belongs to Kuan Yin, to She Who Hears the Cries of the World. And those cries are deafening. As I write, brutal wars and human-caused climate change wreak havoc on our planet. As I write, 110 million war and climate refugees are abandoned without proper homes or safe places. All the bitter fruit of warp-speed patriarchy. All the toxic sludge of identarian politics, strongmen leaders, corrupt governments, and that nefarious 1 percent gobbling up whatever it can wrest from the rest of us.

We have to ask ourselves, do I want to be balm or burden, lover or spoiler, creator or destroyer? Do I want to live split off, separating, and othering? Do I want to live connecting, embracing, and tending our common ground?

If you choose the latter, this chapter is the invitation. And as the poet reminds us, the invitation doesn't say "Come armed with knowledge and a loud voice." It only says "Come."

Understanding that it's not about you, it's about the world, is to say "Yes!" to the invitation. And saying "Yes!" to the invitation is not only hearing the cries of the world. Saying "Yes!" to the invitation is understanding that those cries are your cries too.

People often ask, "How do I keep from drowning in the devastating anguish of the cries of the world? And for that matter, how do I keep from drowning in the brutal fact of my own powerlessness in the presence of those cries?"

I think the answer is in the invitation. I think the answer comes as we open the door. As we say, "Welcome." As we reach across the lines of separation. I think the answer comes as we reach into the ground of love that knows the world as it actually is, which is all one, which is beauty, which is truth, which is more than enough for all, which is awe in the wonder of our everythingness, which is the impeccable splendor.

om srī kuan yin mā

Chapter 20

WORKING WITH THE GODDESS RULES

If you'd like to use these practices as a focus for inner work, here are some suggestions:

- Memorize the Goddess Rules.
- Write them out and hang them in a spot where you'll see them throughout your day.
- Make them into a set of twenty-four cards—four cards for each rule—and pull one every morning. Use this as a contemplation for your day. If you seem to pick the same rule several days in a row, the rule is trying to tell you something. Pay attention.
- Keep a Goddess Rules Journal. Choose one rule each day and use it as a writing prompt.

For additional exercises, prompts, meditations, and mantras, and to join the online community, please visit: **www.suzingreen.com.**

NOTES & CREDITS

To keep this book as reader-friendly as possible, I've opted out of using superscript numbering of the poems and quotes scattered throughout its pages. Notes, permissions, sources, and citations are listed in the order in which they appear.

I'm especially grateful to the poets, their publishers, and agents, who have given me permission to include their work. Every poem I've featured is one I've lived with and loved for many years. This book would not be complete without them. And so to Robert Bly (and Kabir), Andrew Colliver, Daniel Ladinsky (and Hafiz), and Mary Oliver, I am in awe of the wonder of your work, and offer my forever salutations and bowed head.

Epigraph

Excerpts from *The Heart of Awareness: A Translation of the Ashtavakra Gita*, translated by Thomas Byrom. Copyright © 1990 by Thomas Byrom. Reprinted by arrangement with The Permissions Company, LLC on behalf of Shambhala Publications Inc., Boulder, Colorado, shambhala.com., pp. 72–73.

Introduction

"Just sit there," from *The Subject Tonight Is Love: 60 Wild and Sweet Poems of Hafiz* by Daniel Ladinsky © 2003, printed with permission from www.danielladinsky.com., p. 66.

Part I Title Page

This famous quote from Pascal's *Pensées* can be found in Section Two, Fragment 139. Originally published in 1958 by E. P. Dutton & Co., it is now available online via Project Gutenberg. The original line (in English translation) is: *I have discovered that all the unhappiness of men arises from one single fact, that they cannot stay quietly in their own chamber.*

Chapter 1

This wonderful quote is attributed to Laura Simms, a professional storyteller and writer based in NYC. I first saw it in David R. Loy, *The World is Made of Stories* (Somerville, MA: Wisdom Publications, 2010), p. 26. To learn more about her work, please visit: www.laurasimms.com.

Chapter 2

"Crooked Deals," from *The Gift: Poems by Hafiz The Great Sufi Master* by Daniel Ladinsky © 1999 with permission. www.danielladinsky.com., p. 108.

This quote from Bob Dylan is all over the internet, but no source is ever cited. I was reticent to use it without credit; however, after much sleuthing, I found it in a 1969 *Rolling Stone* interview: Jann S. Wenner, "The Rolling Stone Interview: The Elusive Songwriter Goes on the Record" (*Rolling Stone* magazine, November 29, 1969).

"The Idiot's Warehouse," from *The Gift: Poems by Hafiz The Great Sufi Master* by Daniel Ladinsky © 1999 with permission. www.danielladinsky.com, p. 218.

Christina Feldman and Jack Kornfield, editors, *Stories of the Spirit, Stories of the Heart: Parables of the Spiritual Path from Around the World*, (NY: HarperCollins, First Edition, 1991), p. 306.

Chapter 3

Marion Woodman with Jill Mellick, *Coming Home to Myself* (Berkeley, CA: Conari Press, 1998), p. 266. Reprinted with permission from Turner Publishing Company.

Chapter 4

Nor Hall, *The Moon & the Virgin: Reflections on the Archetypal Feminine* (NY: Harper & Row, 1980), p. 68.

Interlude

Diane K. Osbon, editor, *A Joseph Campbell Companion: Reflections on the Art of Living* (NY: HarperCollins, 1991), p. 39.

C.G Jung, The Collected Works of C.G. Jung: Alchemical Studies (NJ: Princeton University Press, 1968, 1983), paragraph 335.

Simone de Beauvoir, *All Said and Done: The Autobiography of Simone de Beauvoir, 1962–1972* (NY: Putnam, 1974).

Chapter 5

Pir Vilayat Inayat Khan, *Thinking Like the Universe: The Sufi Path of Awakening (NY:* Thorsons/HarperCollins, 2000). This quote is often attributed to Pir Vilayat's father, Hazrat Inayat Khan.

Part II Title Page

I first saw this translation of a verse from *Tao Te Ching* in Edward C. Whitmont's *Return of the Goddess* (Continuum Intl. Publishing Group, 1997). Whitmont cites John C.H. Wu's translation of *Tao Te Ching* (NY: St. John's University Press, 1962) as his source.

This statement is part of Sojourner Truth's famous speech, "I Am as Strong as Any Man," delivered at the Women's Rights Convention in Akron, Ohio, on May 29, 1851. The speech is commonly known as "Ain't I a Woman?"

This powerful quote is excerpted from Rebecca Solnit's *The Mother of All Questions* (*Harper's Magazine*, September 30, 2015).

This quote, attributed to Sam Shepard, can be found in memes all over the internet. I've searched his archive and reached out to his publishers and estate. No one has yet been able to source or answer whether Shepard did indeed write or say it. I'll be most grateful for any help in tracking.

Chapter 7

"Between the conscious and the unconscious, the mind has put up a swing," from "Kabir: Ecstatic Poems" by Robert Bly, Copyright © 2004 by Robert Bly. Reprinted by permission of Beacon Press, Boston., p. 18.

Chapter 8

I read Michael Meade's book *Men and the Water of Life* soon after it was published and have been gifting it to the men in my life ever since. Although this quote is all over the internet and attributed to this book, I cannot find it in its pages. I've reached out to Meade's estate for help with sourcing and permissions, but have not yet received a response. For now, the best citation I can offer is: Michael Meade, *Men and the Water of Life: Initiation and the Tempering of Men* (Harper San Francisco, 1993).

Chapter 9

"Mindful" by Mary Oliver. Reprinted by the permission of the Charlotte Sheedy Literary Agency as agent for the author. Copyright © 2004, 2005, 2006, 2017 by Mary Oliver with permission of Bill Reichblum.

These two quotes are from *The Concise Srimad Bhagavatam* (Albany: State University Press of New York, 1989), pp. 374 & 376. Reprinted with permission from the publisher.

Chapter 10

"Good Morning" by Mary Oliver. Reprinted by the permission of the Charlotte Sheedy Literary Agency as agent for the author. Copyright © 2014 by Mary Oliver with permission of Bill Reichblum.

Grace Lee Boggs, *The Next American Revolution: Sustainable Activism for the Twenty-First Century* (Oakland, CA: University of California Press, May 2012), p. 60.

Barbara Ehrenreich, "Time to Wake Up: Stop Blaming Poverty on the Poor" (published in *The Shriver Report: A Woman's Nation Pushes Back from the Brink* in 2014). The entire essay is available on the Center for American Progress archive.

Robert Bly, *A Little Book on the Human Shadow*, edited by William Booth (NY: HarperCollins, 1988), p. 20.

Marion Woodman with Jill Mellick, *Coming Home to Myself* (Berkeley, CA: Conari Press, 1998), p. 92. Reprinted with permission from Turner Publishing Company.

I've seen a handful of translations of the Navajo Blessing Way Ceremony, all of which are similar to this one, and none of which I suspect do it justice. However, even in English, it is sublime.

This Sufi tale is told in Christina Feldman and Jack Kornfield (eds.), *Stories of the Spirit, Stories of the Heart: Parables of the Spiritual Path from Around the World* (NY: Harper Collins, First Edition, 1991), pp. 141–42.

This interview, "Albert Woodfox of Angola 3, Freed After 43 Years in Solitary Confinement," aired on February 22, 2016 on Democracy Now. I've made several requests for permission to reprint this small portion, but have had no response. Please visit www.democracynow.org to listen to the entire interview.

The three quotes from Gregory Boyle are from Gregory Boyle, *Tattoos on the Heart: The Power of Boundless Compassion* (NY: Simon & Schuster: Free Press, 2010), pp. 39, 179, 20. Father Greg is one of my superheroes. If you want to see an example of embodied integration, look no further. Please visit Homeboy Industries (https://homeboyindustries.org/) to support his incredible work.

"Owl Poem" by Mary Oliver. Reprinted by the permission of the Charlotte Sheedy Literary Agency as agent for the author. Copyright © 2014 by Mary Oliver with permission of Bill Reichblum.

"She is Light itself . . ." This quote is excerpted from a slightly longer version I first saw in Ajit Mookerjee, *Kali: The Feminine Force* (Vermont: Destiny Books, 1988), p. 85. Mookerjee credits the source text as *Bhairava Yamala*. I've seen the same quote on websites and in books about the Goddess, always sourced this way. I suspect Mookerjee's book is the source for all of these. I've never been able to find the actual *Bhairava Yamala*. Texts like *Vijnana-Bhairava-Tantra* would seem to include it, but I've not seen it there. The closest I've come to a source is Sir John Woodroffe (Arthur Avalon)'s translation of *Kama-Kala-Vilasa* (*The Splendor or Play of Kama, Desire, and Kala, Creative Power*) but even there, I've seen nothing that mirrors the beauty and power of this quote. So I'm going to leave it in the Mystery and suggest that embodying the Light personified as the Goddess is way more satisfying than reading about it.

Chapter 11

"I Worried" by Mary Oliver. Reprinted by the permission of the Charlotte Sheedy Literary Agency as agent for the author. Copyright © 2010, 2017 by Mary Oliver with permission of Bill Reichblum.

Chapter 12

These lines from the *Lotus Sutra* are excerpted from John Blofeld, *Bodhisattva of Compassion: The Mystical Tradition of Kuan Yin* (Boston: Shambhala Dragon Editions, 1988), p. 108.

Chapter 13

Thomas Wolfe, *You Can't Go Home Again* (NY: Harper & Row, 1940).

Barbara Ehrenreich, *Nickel and Dimed: On (Not) Getting By in America* (NY: Macmillan/Picador, June 1, 2021), p. 221.

Margaret J. Wheatley, *Turning to One Another: Simple Conversations to Restore Hope to the Future* (Oakland, CA: Berrett-Koehler Publishers, February 2, 2009), p. 19.

Marion Woodman and Elinor Dickson, *Dancing in the Flames: The Dark Goddess in the Transformation of Consciousness* (Boston, Shambhala Publications, 1996), p. 174.

Part III Title Page

Starhawk, *The Spiral Dance: A Rebirth of the Ancient Religion of the Great Goddess* (10th Anniversary Edition, Harper & Row, 1989), p. 99. The entire paragraph reads: "The symbolism of the Goddess is not a parallel structure to the symbolism of God the Father. The Goddess does not rule the world; She is the world. Manifest in each of us, She can be known internally by every individual, in all her magnificent diversity."

This quote from Merlin Stone appeared in a *Time* magazine (May 6, 1991) article by Richard Ostling, "When God Was a Woman." The entire quote reads: "'The Goddess is not just the female version of God. She represents a different concept,' says Merlin Stone, author of *When God Was a Woman*. While the Judeo-Christian God is transcendent, the Goddess is located 'within each individual and all things in nature,' she says."

Although this quote is attributed to Terence McKenna, I've searched the archive and reached out to his estate, but have so far been unable find the source.

Chapter 16

"Ten Thousand Idiots," from *The Subject Tonight Is Love: 60 Wild and Sweet Poems of Hafiz* by Daniel Ladinsky, © 2003 with permission. www.daniel-ladinsky.com., p. 51.

Anne Lamott, *Bird by Bird: Some Instructions on Writing and Life* (NY: Pantheon/Random House, 1994), p. 236.

Chapter 17

"Why I Wake Early" by Mary Oliver. Reprinted by the permission of the Charlotte Sheedy Literary Agency as agent for the author. Copyright © 2004, 2005, 2010, 2017 by Mary Oliver with permission of Bill Reichblum.

"This Place Where You Are Right Now," from *The Subject Tonight Is Love: 60 Wild and Sweet Poems of Hafiz* by Daniel Ladinsky, © 2003 with permission. www.danielladinsky.com., p. 12.

"Friend, hope for the Guest while you are alive," from "Kabir: Ecstatic Poems" by Robert Bly, Copyright © 2004 by Robert Bly. Reprinted by permission of Beacon Press, Boston., p. 8-9.

Chapter 18

"What Can I Say" by Mary Oliver. Reprinted by the permission of the Charlotte Sheedy Literary Agency as agent for the author. Copyright © 2010 by Mary Oliver with permission of Bill Reichblum.

Federico Garcia Lorca, *Deep Song and Other Prose* (New York: New Directions, 1980), p. 30.

On Being with Krista Tippett, *Brian Greene: This Tiny Slice of Eternity*, July 15, 2021. Please visit onbeing.org/programs.

Chapter 19

I fell in love with the poem "Come" when I first saw it on Ivan Granger's Poetry Chaikhana website many years ago. I've read it at numerous classes, workshops, and retreats and it always brings the house down. I think it is the perfect poem to bless the final chapter of this book and am forever grateful to the poet Andrew Colliver for allowing me to use it here.

Although still unpublished when I discovered it, "Come" is now included in the 2018 Poetry Chaikhana Anthology, *This Dance of Bliss: Ecstatic Poetry from Around the World*, edited with Commentary by Ivan M. Granger. If you're interested in sacred poetry, Poetry Chaikhana is the go-to source. (https://www.poetry-chaikhana.com/)

COUNTING MY BLESSINGS AND CLEANING MY HOUSE

I started writing this book on Valentine's Day 2019, and it has truly been a labor of love. While writing is, in many ways, a solo journey, I've had great company along the way. To the Monday Night crew: Abigail, Alison, Caron, Claude, Raquel, and Shawn, and to my daughter, Coby—you are midwives to this book. You cheered me on from the beginning, read PDFs and printouts of the work in progress, listened to me read chapters out loud, believed in what I have to say, pushed me to say it better, and offered me unwavering love, joy, and support. I could never have written this book without you. Thank you from the bottom of my heart.

To dear friends, family, and extended family, you have been here in the most important ways: Alison and Andy; Carole B.; Caron and Chet; Claude and Dan; David and Kerry; my sister, Deborah; Daniel J.; Eric H.; Francine L.; Gregg A.; Lisha and Shawn; Marcel and Sujata; my niece, Marissa; Raquel and Jim; Robert M.; and my son-in-law, Keith, who provided brilliant media services and unflagging IT support.

To the literary world professionals whose combined expertise helped me shepherd this book through its journey of becoming: Elizabeth Brown, Jane Cavolina, Libby Jordan, Julia Pastore, and Jesseca Salkey; to Jude Berman and Fran McManus, sister writers who are always there when I need a hand; and to the team at She

Writes Press, who turned my dream of a book into the object you hold in your hands.

And finally, to my twenty-something cohort: Jasper, Juliette, and Mia. You dear ones keep me young, connected, and most of all, give me hope for the future.

ABOUT THE AUTHOR

Photo credit: Keith Pyatt

Suzin Green is a writer, musician, wisdom teacher, and therapist whose work bridges Eastern philosophy, Western psychology, and the arts. A pioneer in Expressive Arts Therapy and Meditation-Based Life Coaching, she is also the creator of *The Mantra Project*, a celebrated series of music albums inspired by ancient yogic chant. For decades, Suzin has guided students and clients seeking greater depth and meaning in their lives. She currently lives in New Jersey where, when not working, she can be found walking, tending her garden, or doting on her cat.

The Goddess Remedy reflects the essence of her life's work—offering a fresh perspective on the goddess, not as a distant archetype but as a living connection to the unifying power of love.

Looking for your next great read?

We can help!

Visit www.shewritespress.com/next-read
or scan the QR code below for a list
of our recommended titles.

She Writes Press is an award-winning
independent publishing company founded to
serve women writers everywhere.